Beautifully Unique
Sparkleponies

Beautifully Unique Sparkleponies

ON MYTHS, MORONS, FREE SPEECH, FOOTBALL, AND ASSORTED ABSURDITIES

Chris Kluwe

LITTLE, BROWN AND COMPANY
New York • Boston • London

Little, Brown and Company
Hachette Book Group
237 Park Avenue, New York, NY 10017
littlebrown.com

First Edition: June 2013

Little, Brown and Company is a division of Hachette Book Group, Inc. The Little, Brown name and logo are trademarks of Hachette Book Group, Inc.

The publisher is not responsible for websites (or their content) that are not owned by the publisher.

The Hachette Speakers Bureau provides a wide range of authors for speaking events. To find out more, go to hachettespeakersbureau.com or call (866) 376-6591.

ISBN 978-0-316-23677-5
LCCN 2013935097

10 9 8 7 6 5 4 3 2 1

RRD-C

Printed in the United States of America

To my family,
to my friends,
to my teachers,
to my editors,
and to everyone who helped with everything
I cannot do on my own,
Thank You

Contents

Contents

Contents

Beautifully Unique
Sparkleponies

Hello?

I've decided to call my own mind. There's a lot of different characters in there, and I think we need to talk. Sadly, I have to use my three-year-old phone with crappy reception because I'm too cheap to upgrade to one that actually works, but I guess that's on me.

First up is Football. As the phone rings, I pace around like a lion on methadone. I've never been able to sit still while I'm on the phone; it seems like thinking and listening and talking with someone I can't see causes me to fill in the gaps with movement. Sometimes my wife yells at me because I'm driving her to distraction. I hope she doesn't Tase me one day.

Football finally picks up. I can hear the yelling of coaches in the background. How's it going? I ask. Oh, just fine, Football responds. It's the usual—sitting around during practice thinking of spaceships, video-game ideas, possible book topics, how many different shades of blue there are before you start entering green—anything at all, really, to keep from going violently insane after we finish the forty-five minutes of punting we're here for.

A dull roar shakes the phone in my ear—it sounds like a plane just landed on Football's head. What was that? Inthemiddle ofagamehavetogothesnapiscomingpuntisoffgottacoverherecomes hesterohshitohshitoh—*click*. The phone goes dead, the call cut off. I shrug and dial the number for Reading.

Reading doesn't pick up, usually never does. Spends all its time among stacks of books, science fiction and fantasy mainly, tuning everything out inside the hushed cathedral silence of a library. I'm never quite sure where I'm going to go with Reading, but it's always a great trip. I swear, though, if Reading ever gets an e-reader, I'm going to lobotomize myself. You can't beat the feel of paper on fingertips.

Next on the list is abstract. I dial the number, and my phone swallows me up and spits me *out inside a psychedelic landscape of non-Euclidean geometry and fireworks. The colors taste like triangles. All of a sudden, a herd of bowling-ball llamas run past me whispering scenes from* Hamlet *while a thunderous bass track shimmers the air into crystal sculptures. At one point, I'm pretty sure they all look like Jessica Rabbit. Commence the sweet-tea tango.* <record scratch>

Time to leave, before abstract takes me on another tangent. It's a fun place to visit, interesting scenery, but I don't think I'd want to live there.

At this point I realize I'm talking to Reason. Reason's always sitting above everything else, *custodiet* the custodians and all that, and usually keeps abstract on a pretty tight leash. There's a couple long-chain molecular compounds that can distract Reason for a while, but they also generally make the next morning slightly unpleasant, so they get in only occasionally. The funny thing, though, is that Reason is the only one that will let them in in the first place. Unless Reason's satisfied that it's okay to take a break, all guards stay on high alert.

Reason assures me that it's still very much in control at the moment, so I hang up and go looking for the last portion of my mind I'd like to speak with. It crafts me a wonderful conversation and then brings this snapshot to a close.

Enjoy the ride.

Welcome to the Circus

I never intended to write a book. All of this started when I wrote a letter.

A lot of people seemed to enjoy reading this letter, and one of the reasons they enjoyed reading it was that it had a bunch of naughty words in it. Words like *lustful cockmonster* and *narcissistic fromunda stain* and *holy fucking shitballs*.

Some other people didn't like the language, and I imagine they went into apoplectic fits when they finally reached the very last word I wrote down, which I've taken the delight of reprinting here:

Asshole.

Coincidentally, Kurt Vonnegut always included a stylized picture of an asshole next to his signature (one of the many delightful hand-drawn illustrations he liked to include in his stories). There's a big asterisk middle finger emblazoned on the spine of each book (at least on the ones I own, anyway), telling the world that this was his voice and you could take it or leave it.

I like Kurt's voice, how he was able to highlight the absurdities and awfulness of the human race, hope and depression all twisted together into one complex knot (just like people!). I'm not Kurt, though. I have to use my own voice — colorful language, obscure tangents, mixed metaphors, and all.

As the great poet Marshall Mathers put it,

Sorry, Mama, I'm grown, I must travel alone
Ain't following no footsteps, I'm making my own.

Ladies and gentlemen, start your engines.

So now that I'm writing a book, people have suggested topics for me to consider. Some of them I like, some of them I'll ignore (I'm the one writing; I get to make the rules), but one in particular I find absolutely fascinating. The topic is "How the truth will always help you win."

Sorry, but that's not true. The truth will help you win only if people are willing to educate themselves as to *why* truth is important, and, make no mistake, truth is very important.

But what is truth?

To me, truth boils down to two things: a willingness to see the world as it really is, and the desire to change your beliefs when they conflict with your vision.

First off, to see the world as it really is. The world, one that we've made for ourselves, is absolutely fucked. We drop bombs on each other, kill children in the name of religion, discriminate against the poor and minorities because they're "different," pollute and destroy and despoil to satisfy our own selfish needs; in short, human beings are assholes.

The world is also full of joy and wonder: a fireman running into a burning building to save a complete stranger; a church offering food and shelter to the homeless; a child given encouragement and love from those around her. Human beings are assholes, but they're also self-sacrificing, noble, and filled with boundless love.

The world is full of complexity. This is the truth, and it's a hard one to learn. People can't be defined by labels or categories; one man's hero is another man's villain. We cannot judge people by their own claims, which they shape as they see fit, or their thoughts, which we cannot see; we can judge people only by their actions and by how those actions affect others around them.

The truth is that the world is what we make it. What consequences our actions bring—that is truth. What our society values, not in word or phrase but in law and policy—that is truth. What people are willing to fight for, work for, die for—that is truth. The only truth that is self-evident is that we determine how truthful we want to be with each other.

Right now, the truth is that we value the shallow, the immaterial, the worthless, and the inane. Huge department stores and horse-meat hamburger chains are built on shoveling as much cheap, easily replaceable trash on people as they can, no matter the consequences. (Have another Double McLard Burger to go with your lead-infused milk!) Reality TV, daytime talk shows— they're mindless pap to distract us from actual issues. (But, boy, I'm sure glad Maury found out the fifth man tested was the child's father!) Political races are closer to gladiatorial spectacles than rational discussions of important matters (why think when we can be entertained!).

The truth will always help you win? Hardly likely. No one is interested in the truth anymore, because the truth is harsh, unpalatable, bitter to the tongue and the mind. Give us our soma, our video walls, our bread and circuses to numb the dull ache of ignorance until we don't even realize what it is we've lost. Give us *a* truth, but not *the* truth, because to change our beliefs and confront that truth is to admit that we've failed as a country and as a people, grown fat and indolent on the spoils of empire, that we're content to fiddle as it all slowly burns around us, unwilling and unable to recognize that this path has been well trod throughout the course of history. For the truth to win, you have to *want* to know the truth, and not many people have the appetite.

Perhaps enough people will one day realize the truth—that we have only each other on this planet, that how we treat one another is the only legacy we leave for our children—and will act accordingly. Perhaps one day people will realize that we are a species composed of complex and unique individuals, that our differences don't divide us but instead highlight our wondrous diversity. Perhaps one day people will treat each other the way they want to be treated: with respect, with dignity, with tolerance and compassion. That's the day the truth will win.

Until that day, ask me no questions, and I'll tell you no lies.

Some People Don't Understand Logic

Emmett C. Burns is a Maryland state delegate who, in August 2012, wrote a letter to the owner of the Baltimore Ravens concerning statements made by Ravens linebacker Brendon Ayanbadejo in favor of same-sex marriage. The letter from Mr. Burns (n'excellent) to the Ravens demanded the organization inhibit Brendon's right to free speech, which I had a bit of a problem with. In response, I wrote this letter, which originally appeared on Deadspin, *because they'll print just about anything (love you guys).*

Dear Emmett C. Burns Jr.,

I find it inconceivable that you are an elected official of Maryland's state government. Your vitriolic hatred and bigotry make me ashamed and disgusted to think that you are in any way responsible for shaping policy at any level. The views you espouse neglect to consider several fundamental key points, which I will outline in great detail (you may want to hire an intern to help you with the longer words):

1. As I suspect you have not read the Constitution, I would like to remind you that the very first, the VERY FIRST, amendment in this founding document deals with the freedom of speech, particularly the abridgment of said freedom. By using your position as an elected official (when referring to your constituents so as to implicitly threaten the Ravens organization) to state that the Ravens should "inhibit such expressions from your employees," more specifically Brendon Ayanbadejo, not only are you clearly violating the First Amendment, you also come across as a narcissistic fromunda stain. What on earth would possess you to be so mind-bogglingly stupid? It baffles me that a man such as yourself, a man who relies on that same First Amendment to pursue your own religious studies without fear of persecution from the state, could somehow justify stifling another person's right to speech. To call that *hypocritical* would be to do a disservice to the word. *Mindfucking obscenely hypocritical* starts to approach it a little bit.

2. "Many of your fans are opposed to such a view and feel it has no place in a sport that is strictly for pride, entertainment, and excitement." Holy fucking shitballs. Did you seriously just say that, as someone who's "deeply involved in government task forces on the legacy of slavery in Maryland"? Have you not heard of Kenny Washington? Jackie Robinson? As recently as 1962 the NFL still had segregation, which was only done away with by

brave athletes and coaches daring to speak their mind and do the right thing, and you're going to say that political views have "no place in a sport"? I can't even begin to fathom the cognitive dissonance that must be coursing through your rapidly addled mind right now; the mental gymnastics your brain has to tortuously contort itself through to make such a preposterous statement are surely worthy of an Olympic gold medal (the Russian judge gives you a 10 for "beautiful oppressionism").

3. This is more a personal quibble of mine, but why do you hate freedom? Why do you hate the fact that other people want a chance to live their lives and be happy, even though they may believe in something different than you, or act different than you? How does gay marriage, in any way, shape, or form, affect your life? If gay marriage becomes legal, are you worried that all of a sudden you'll start thinking about penis? "Oh shit. Gay marriage just passed. Gotta get me some of that hot dong action!" Will all of your friends suddenly turn gay and refuse to come to your Sunday Ticket grill-outs? (Unlikely, since gay people enjoy watching football too.)

I can assure you that gay people getting married will have zero effect on your life. They won't come into your house and steal your children. They won't magically turn you into a lustful cockmonster. They won't even overthrow the government in an orgy of hedonistic debauchery because all of a sudden they have the same legal rights as the other 90 percent of our population—rights like Social Security benefits, child-care tax credits, Family and Medical Leave to take care of loved ones, and COBRA health care for spouses and children. You know what having these rights will make gays? Full-fledged American citizens just like everyone else, with the freedom to pursue happiness and all that entails. Do the civil-rights struggles of the past two hundred years mean absolutely nothing to you?

In closing, I would like to say that I hope this letter, in some small way, causes you to reflect upon the magnitude of the colossal foot-in-mouth clusterfuck you so brazenly unleashed on a man whose only crime was speaking out for something he believed in. Best of luck in the next election; I'm fairly certain you might need it.

Sincerely,
Chris Kluwe

PS: I've also been vocal as hell about the issue of gay marriage so you can take your "I know of no other NFL player who has done what Mr. Ayanbadejo is doing" and shove it in your close-minded, totally-lacking-in-empathy piehole and choke on it. Asshole.

Bowdlerizations

First off, let me say thank you to all the people who commented on my letter to Emmett C. Burns Jr.

You all give me great hope for the human race—hope that one day we can rise up past the petty differences that divide us and realize we're all in this together. Perhaps our children won't look back on our stewardship with regret.

Second, I heard from quite a few sources (including my dad) that the letter would have been more powerful and would have delivered the message better without the swearing, and that those who would refute the point could seize upon my colorful insults to dismiss the main thrust as little more than childish antics and egotistical displays of temper.

Bollocks.

The swearing is there for a reason. What Emmett C. Burns Jr. wrote, what I responded to, was far more disgusting and foul-minded than any simple scatological reference or genital mash-up. His words degrade the very essence of the English language with their barely hidden venom and intolerant hate; drag it screaming into the muck of iniquity by wrapping a mantle of seeming reasonableness around corruption and control; masquerade as discourse while screaming their very lies to any heaven you care to name — I could go on.

My words? My words are a litmus test for those who would see the truth of a message rather than the package it's delivered in. I won't lie; I use those words also because I personally find them entertaining to write and read (as do a large number of other people), but those who argue that my message means nothing simply because I'm referencing a portion of the male anatomy would never have accepted the message anyway. They would have used other excuses to refute it, like "Oh, he's just a punter," or "What do you know? You just play football," or "No one cares what you think, you fag."

No, my words are meant for those who might be on the fence, those who are initially drawn in due to shock, or laughter, or outrage but then look at what lies beneath, at the truth of the matter. Those people I might reach, might give a quick lightbulb flicker of "Ohhh, so that's what's wrong with that argument." But those who don't look, who don't question, who happily treat the symptoms and not the disease — isn't that the very problem with our politics today? No one is interested in what lies hidden in plain sight beneath what's said, the glossy dung ball of intolerance and hate buffed to a lustrous gleam by rhetoric and catchphrases.

So here is my gift to you. The exact same letter, but without the oh-so-naughty words, which only mean what we allow them to mean. What will your excuse be this time?

*   *   *

Dear Emmett C. Burns Jr.,

I find it inconceivable that you are an elected official of Maryland's state government. Your vitriolic hatred and bigotry make me ashamed and disgusted to think that you are in any way responsible for shaping policy at any level. The views you espouse neglect to consider several fundamental key points, which I will outline in great detail (you may want to hire an intern to help you with the longer words):

1. As I suspect you have not read the Constitution, I would like to remind you that the very first, the VERY FIRST, amendment in this founding document deals with the freedom of speech, particularly the abridgment of said freedom. By using your position as an elected official (when referring to your constituents so as to implicitly threaten the Ravens organization) to state that the Ravens should "inhibit such expressions from your employees," more specifically Brendon Ayanbadejo, not only are you clearly violating the First Amendment, you also come across as a BEAUTIFULLY UNIQUE SPARKLEPONY. What on earth would possess you to be so mind-bogglingly stupid? It baffles me that a man such as yourself, a man who relies on that same First Amendment to pursue your own religious studies without fear of persecution from the state, could somehow justify stifling another person's right to speech. To call that *hypocritical* would be to do a disservice to the word. *SAD-PUPPY-DOG-EYES hypocritical* starts to approach it a little bit.

2. "Many of your fans are opposed to such a view and feel it has no place in a sport that is strictly for pride, entertainment, and excitement." *DISAPPOINTED LEMUR FACE WITH SOLITARY TEAR TRICKLING DOWN TO CHIN.* Did you

seriously just say that, as someone who's "deeply involved in government task forces on the legacy of slavery in Maryland"? Have you not heard of Kenny Washington? Jackie Robinson? As recently as 1962, the NFL still had segregation, which was only done away with by brave athletes and coaches daring to speak their mind and do the right thing, and you're going to say that political views have "no place in a sport"? I can't even begin to fathom the cognitive dissonance that must be coursing through your rapidly addled mind right now; the mental gymnastics your brain has to tortuously contort itself through to make such a preposterous statement are surely worthy of an Olympic gold medal (the Russian judge gives you a 10 for "beautiful oppressionism").

3. This is more a personal quibble of mine, but why do you hate freedom? Why do you hate the fact that other people want a chance to live their lives and be happy, even though they may believe in something different than you, or act different than you? How does gay marriage, in any way, shape, or form, affect your life? If gay marriage becomes legal, are you worried that all of a sudden you'll start thinking about DANCING CHUB-TOAD? "ALACK AND ALAS MY TOP HAT HAS FALLEN. Gay marriage just passed. Gotta get me some of that DELICIOUS STATE FAIR HOT DOG!" Will all of your friends suddenly turn gay and refuse to come to your Sunday Ticket grill-outs? (Unlikely, since gay people enjoy watching football too.)

I can assure you that gay people getting married will have zero effect on your life. They won't come into your house and steal your children. They won't magically turn you into a lustful FROLICKING OSTRICH. They won't even overthrow the government in an orgy of hedonistic debauchery because all of a sudden they have the same legal rights as the other 90 percent of our population, rights like Social Security benefits, child-care tax credits, Family and Medical Leave to take care of loved ones, and COBRA health care for spouses and children. You know what having these rights will make gays? Full-fledged American citizens just like everyone else, with the freedom to pursue happiness and all that entails. Do the civil-rights struggles of the past two hundred years mean absolutely nothing to you?

In closing, I would like to say that I hope this letter, in some small way, causes you to reflect upon the magnitude of the colossal foot-in-mouth SLIDE WHISTLE TO E-FLAT you so brazenly unleashed on a man whose only crime was speaking out for something he believed in. Best of luck in the next election; I'm fairly certain you might need it.

Sincerely,
Chris Kluwe

PS: I've also been vocal as hell about the issue of gay marriage so you can take your "I know of no other NFL player who has done what Mr. Ayanbadejo is doing" and shove it in your close-minded, totally-lacking-in-empathy piehole and choke on it. UNFORTUNATELY PHALLIC HEDGE SCULPTURE.

A Letter to Jesus

Dear Jesus,

Can you believe this shit? All around the world, people are claiming that your words give them the right to kill, maim, and torture each other. It's like they've totally forgotten why you went up on that cross in the first place! They're completely ignoring the fact that you took all that sin and suffering upon yourself so we could have a chance at redemption and not make the same mistakes again and again.

How are things with you and Muhammad in Heaven? You both had a vision of something better here on Earth, but look at the absolute clusterfuck we've made of it. No one wants to follow your examples anymore; instead, they look for words written by other men and use them to justify whatever it is they want to believe. When was the last time you guys personally preached hate, or fear? (And no, I'm not talking about your apostles and followers; those poopstains are in it for themselves.)

When was the last time someone looked at the actual content of your message? Self-sacrifice instead of sacrificing others. Loving your neighbor as yourself, and not loving his car or his wife. Charity to the meek and the poor, not the boastful and rich. How can you even stand to look at the world anymore without closing your eyes in the most epic of face-palms?

Also, can you guys do something about the organized part of religion? I'm pretty sure that suicide bombers and child molesters weren't in the game plan you two left behind, nor were palaces and worldly power. Why don't people pay more attention to the parts about love and kindness and less to the archaic rules and regulations that don't even make sense anymore? Also, seriously, how much do you want to giggle every time you see the pope hat?

What are your thoughts on cell phones, Jesus? I notice that nowhere in the Bible do you talk about cell phones, and I'm really kind of curious what your take on them is. Same with the Internet. Can you imagine being a messiah with access to the Internet? Well, of course you can imagine it, what with the whole Son of God thing, but I'm telling you, it would be amazing if you reappeared today. There'd be nothing but "LOL-JESUS" and "I CAN HAZ SALVATION?" memes across every single message board. Honestly, I'm pretty sure your actual message would get down-voted and ignored; sure, you might get a comment or two on Reddit, but that would be it. I doubt you'd even make the front page of anything other than Christ-SpearThrust.gif.

Well, Jesus, I guess in closing, I'd like to say that it's a good thing you aren't around today. I can't imagine you'd be very happy with all the people co-opting your love and tolerance to preach hate and discrimination; I'm pretty sure you kicked over a moneylender's stall or two the last time you saw that happening (if you wanted to head over to Wall Street right now, though, I don't think there'd be a lot of sad faces). Here's hoping that our next millennium turns out better than the last one!

Sincerely,
An Unwashed Heathen

That Dark Passenger

Losing sucks. It's the absolute worst feeling in the world, and anyone who tells you that losing is okay is lying to both you and himself. The sensation is like a colony of fire ants gnawing away at your inner abdominals, spitting their venom all over your insides until you feel you have to scream to release the pain. You put in hours of effort during the week practicing the same stupid motions and plays over and over, and then, after time runs out and the lights go off, you're left with nothing but an aching sense of hurt and regret.

Nothing you fans say to us will make us feel worse than what we're already saying to ourselves. "You're a loser," "You guys suck," "Why don't you practice more?"; these are nothing compared to the internal monologue of someone who has ferociously competed for a win and come up short. It doesn't matter what the player's job is or how much he played; when the team fails to win, it's on all of you, and all of you feel like crap. *What could I have done better? Where could I have made more of a difference? Why didn't I execute that job perfectly?* All these and more are running endless circles through our minds, a ceaseless train of mocking self-loathing.

But we can't show it. We can't acknowledge it, can't give voice to it, can't let the bitter sting of defeat shout its pain to the world, because we have to get ready for next week.

Players have to take all those voices, all those nasty little thoughts, and wall them off behind mental barriers so high and thick they make the Great Wall of China look like a sand castle at high tide. You have to push it aside and do your best to forget the pain even exists, because if you let it affect the outcome of the next game, that deadly spiral will crush you until there's nothing left but bitter regrets and shattered dreams. You have to believe that you can move on and forget the past, because there's not one damn thing you can do to change it now; actions have been performed and judged and found wanting—your effort and intent was simply not good enough that day.

It fades after a while, the angry introspection of defeat, but it's always there, always lurking in that mental prison, pacing restlessly behind its bars like a caged tiger, eyes agleam with savage hunger to rend and tear. You can never let that beast out, though, lest it wreak havoc on your life and on the lives of those around you. Some placate it with alcohol; some with religion; some with sex; some even tame it with the hard-earned serenity of acceptance, the realization that what's done is done and no one can change the past no matter how much it hurts.

So while we may put on brave faces and tell you, "This game's behind us, we're focusing on next week," don't ever make the mistake of thinking that we don't care, that we don't feel the loss a hundred times more keenly than you do. Don't think that it doesn't add up over the weeks and years until sometimes we want to rage at the world at the top of our lungs.

We're just better at hiding it than you are.

The Rush

I've been very fortunate in my life to have experienced something very few people get to experience—the adrenaline thrill of performing my job in front of thousands of screaming people in a stadium and millions more watching on television, almost all of whom would die happy if they could live my life for one day. What does it feel like? Nervousness, confidence, elation, despair, humility, pride—a thousand conflicting feelings coursing torrentially through my body and mind.

What does it feel like? A small candlelit bubble of self drifting in a dark and terrible sea.

Standing on the sideline is where it starts. I can feel a tight knot begin to form in my stomach, the onset of nerves, but that's normal, and I push it to the side. There's no way not to get nervous, and anyone who tells you otherwise is lying to you or to himself. The trick is to ignore it, because if you can't, you'll never make it at this level. Sure, all eyes are on you, and everyone will know if you make a mistake, but that can't be your focus. You have to be locked in on one thing, and one thing only — doing your job to the utmost of your ability. And if you don't, you're going to get fired. Try not to think about that either, if you can help it.

Breathe! That's the rookie mistake most people make. When your body engages in the primal fight-or-flight response, you draw shorter, faster breaths, which is a problem, since you need all the oxygen you can get when it's time to perform. I find that several deep inhalations calm the adrenaline tremors twitching my limbs and help me relax into the routine of playing. A day job that's unlike any other day job in the world. Fourth down inevitably rolls around, and it's time to get to work.

I jog out onto the field, and the shouts of the crowd surrounding me fade away into a dull roar, an ocean of sound I float atop. Some days the tide is angry, all-consuming — torrents of white noise crashing over and through me like foaming breakers in the midst of storm-racked skies. Other days are calm and still, the scattered cries of individual fans piercing the air like the shrill cries of birds squabbling over a fish. Through it all, I remain focused on one thing: catching the football and executing the best punt I can, expecting, hoping for, success.

Check the ball placement, toes lined up thirteen and a half yards away, left foot staggered slightly in front of right, weight balanced evenly near the balls of my feet in case I need to adjust to a snap. Wipe hands on pants to ensure best catching surface; raise and loosely extend them to give my long-snapper a target to aim at. Focus on the tip of the ball as the snapper adjusts it in his pre-snap routine, block out everything else as best as I'm able;

players blur into barely felt presences on the edges of my peripheral vision.

A sudden intake of breath, ball spinning back, violent explosions of motion off in the far distance as titans grapple and twist.

Time slows down to molasses, syrupy thick and clinging.

Watch the ball in for the catch, every tactile surface immediately feeling for laces as a reference point, hands twisting and turning to adjust it into the proper drop plane, middle finger supporting the bottom seam while palm and thumb complete the pyramid base, left hand guiding and stabilizing oh so briefly before rising up to balance the whiplash strike of kicking that seems so far away; *now* ball lightly weighing down my right hand as I bring it to waist level; *now* right foot lands and left foot begins its balanced stride forward, not too short, not too long; *now* right arm gradually extends (keeping a slight bend in the elbow, to prevent the drop from crossing inside) and then falls away, letting the ball float freely for the barest instant as my left foot locks into the ground and all the muscles on my right lower side contract and then explode up through an expelled grunt of air, left arm fully outstretched to the sky, eyes never leaving the gold *Wilson* engraved on the side, though they're not quick enough to actually see the moment of impact, *and now* I'm following through and time returns to normal again, an eternity of 1.2 seconds later.

Bodies rush and whir past like frenzied tops, and it's time to start running downfield, legs churning and arms pumping, scanning for the returner, for possible seams to fill, for potential blockers to avoid (I've been blindsided a couple times, and it never feels good). Time starts moving faster at this point, too much chaotic motion for me to focus on any one thing; frozen instants are all that register.

There—a gunner makes a diving grab as the returner twists and eels free.

There—a wing gets pushed to the side by an opponent, daylight momentarily flashing as the returner sprints for a rapidly closing gap.

There—I step around a blocker and find myself within arm's reach of the returner, both of us moving in the same plane of vectors for the briefest of moments.

There—I stick an arm out and latch on, spinning-tumbling-bouncing through the air and off the ground, a whirlwind kaleidoscope blurring around me until we slide to a halt and the whistles blow.

I pick myself up off the ground and jog back over to the sideline. Barely twenty seconds have elapsed since I walked onto the field, but it feels like twenty minutes. If it was a bad kick, I mentally beat myself up in a fit of pure rage and then make it melt away like summer snow—time to focus on the next kick. If it was a good kick, I allow myself a fiery moment of exultation and triumph before I tamp it down to gently glowing coals—time to focus on the next kick.

The rush of crowd noise, drifting and dying away.

The rush of adrenaline, sacrificial fuel offered and consumed.

The rush of bodies, avoided and ignored.

The rush of time, accepted and embraced.

The rush of the waves, in, out, in—bubbles drifting serenely off into the distance.

A thin reed, a rush, but one that weathers all storms.

Mirror, Mirror

I have no tolerance for bigots. I have no tolerance for sexists. I have no tolerance for racists, would-be slave owners, or those who would oppress another group simply because they can. I have absolutely NO tolerance for those who don't treat other people the way they would want to be treated. I have nothing but contempt for those who would pass a constitutional amendment *denying* equality under the law to a segment of American citizens. We've fought countless battles over the years trying to bring greater equality to both this country and the world, and they would shove it aside like so much trash.

And guess what: My intolerance doesn't kick in until YOU do something. Treat everyone equally and with respect, and we'll never have a problem. Unfortunately, some people just don't get it.

I won't sugarcoat it, won't hide it in fancy words, won't wrap it in a swaddling of morality and fear: If you vote to restrict the rights of other people, you are trying to make them your slaves. You are telling them that the very birthright that makes us human, the right to free will and choice, the right to happiness and freedom, does not apply to them. You are flat-out stating that these people are no longer human beings, that YOU should decide what's best, with no care for independent thought, that YOU alone know the only way to do things.

I call this oppression. I call it tyranny. I call it cruel and unjust and undeserving of consideration by anyone who would live free of shackles. America, the America I was brought up in, the America I want my children to live in, is a land of *inclusion*, not *exclusion*. " 'Give me your tired, your poor, your huddled masses yearning to breathe free.' " There's no addendum to the Statue of Liberty plaque that says "But hey, fags, get the JACKBOOT TO BACKSIDE out. Blacks, we don't want you either. Muslims, Buddhists, Jews, don't even think about it." This country was built on the idea that everyone is equal under the law, everyone deserves the same rights and respect of free will, everyone can pursue happiness. I will happily lay down my life to protect your right to *believe* whatever you want, but when your *actions* are oppressive, we're gonna have some problems, because now you've crossed the line dividing your free will from someone else's. There is only one thing I will not allow in my life, and that is an action that tolerates discrimination.

I am completely intolerant of intolerance. Any time someone uses his opinion to enforce actions that oppress a segment of the population, I'll be right there giving the biggest middle finger I can find. Any time someone thinks she has the right to pass laws that take away another person's free will, I'll be shouting profanity at the top of my lungs. Any time someone believes that life should be corralled and constrained, that actions between con-senting adults that cause no harm to others should be legislated away, that the enslavement of humanity is somehow a good thing, then, by any god you care to name, I will raise my voice and call out your arrogant FLIES CIRCLING COWPAT from every single rooftop I can find.

Here's the thing: I really don't care what your personal opin-ion is on anything. If you want to believe that the Flying Spaghetti Monster will condemn us all to the Molten Mozzarella Pits for not sacrificing daily at its altar, more power to you! If you want to believe gay people getting married will usher in an eternal age of terror, that's your choice to make (I may not agree with the choice, but it's yours). But the instant, the very instant you change that opinion into an action—the moment you make laws forcing someone to worship at your altar, or restricting people's right to marry whom they want, or taking away freedoms and protections due to skin color or sexuality; that coldly self-involved second when you treat me (or anyone else) as a thing, as an object, as a slave with no right to self-determination or free will—well, my friend, that's when my intolerance kicks into high gear.

Let me tell you a little story about mirrors. When you look into a mirror, every reflected action comes from one source—you. That person you see looking back at you will treat you exactly how you treat him. If you smile, or wave, or laugh, the reflection reacts with appropriate good cheer. Make angry faces or scream, and you quickly find yourself the subject of every barb and indig-nity you're trying to heap upon the shoulders of another. If you find yourself bristling under the scorn, the contempt, the lack of respect, don't blame the mirror. All it's reflecting is you.

The Darkness and the Light

Tonight I was lying in bed trying to think up a solid way to launch into an exploration of the traveling life of a football player as my wife watched her shows on the DVR (*Big Bang Theory,* the *Daily Show, Modern Family,* and the *Colbert Report,* for those interested). Basically, I wanted to write something about how I fly all over the country but I pretty much see only the interiors of hotel rooms and locker rooms; name a tourist trap I'd enjoy checking out, and I probably have no idea what you're talking about.

Then, as I got into the piece, I realized I needed to do some traveling of a different sort—I had to move from the bed because I was getting distracted by the TV (I enjoy listening as my wife watches, but it tends to focus my concentration toward the TV and away from the writing).

Luckily, since I write on a laptop, moving to the family room was accomplished with relative ease and minimal spousal strife, affording me ample solitude to work on the traveling piece. Sitting on the couch with the lights off, the monitor glow my lone island of illumination, focused fully on the task at hand, I was ready to start deriving meaning from formlessness.

Only now I wanted to write about something else.

I was suddenly reminded of a picture I had seen on Twitter several days before. It was of author Neil Gaiman curled up on his couch writing a new Sandman book (if you haven't read the Sandman series, you should; they're awesome graphic novels) in the dark—and it amazed me how similarly the creative process was playing out for me.

I knew I wasn't going to write about flying; I wanted to write about writing (how meta!).

Alone in the dark with only my thoughts, no outside distractions creeping in, my own private interpretation of the universe ready to spring forth from my mind, awaiting only the proper electrical impulses to transfer thought into action—is this what all writers, all spinners of fables and yarns, crave? That tiny darkness inside our heads that envelops the spark of imagination, itself surrounded by the sensory deprivation we need while we go about the act of creation? Do we subconsciously harken back to the primal days of our ancestors as they gathered around the campfire while unseen creatures' noises echoed through an undefined night?

It's as though we're ancient men, travelers in a hostile world, slaves to our environment, spinning tales of Fox and Coyote (Trickster!), Lion and Bear (Strength!), Owl and Crow (Wisdom!) as shadows beat at the edges of flickering light, telling stories that, perhaps, can cage the darkness surrounding us, give it a name, make knowable the unknown.

Is that what we as writers look for? The mad unknown? The

huge, hazy shapes of ideas our minds long to grasp, the wriggling words we try to pin on transient mediums? Is that why many of us, consciously or not, re-create that same prototypical world, the physical darkness all around? In order to communicate in a shared language every one of us upright apes instinctually understands, the language of concept and metaphor?

(I wish I could accurately describe how difficult it is to get thoughts from my head onto the screen in front of me when it comes to ideas like this. The best way I can describe it is it's like trying to wrestle a fog bank into a condensed ball; I'm constantly trying to corral and define the edges in order to create a recognizable shape, and it fights back at every turn. Seriously, in my head, I just went from football and television pop culture to the metaphysical roots of how stories are told. The darkness does not give up its secrets easily.)

When trying to write, many people never go looking for that primal act of creation, that tiny spark amid a roiling sea of black. Instead, they shut out the world within them, drown it in the glitzy flash of blinking lights and empty noise, banish it beneath the harsh glare of outrospection. Someone sits down to craft a novel, or a play, or a movie, or even a Tweet, but he gets distracted by the mundanity around him, the sheer overwhelming chaos of it all (which is not to say that you can't write while listening to music or whatever; I've just noticed that when I do that, it's a lot harder and the writing tends to be more about the influences around me).

Or, worst of all, someone stops writing because he listens to that tiny voice that says, *What you're writing isn't any good because someone else has already said it.*

Well, you shouldn't listen to that voice, because while it's partially right, it's also wrong. The stories we craft, the webs we weave, they are all drawn from the same common threads scattered throughout our shared histories. There's no such thing as originality in the components of a story—our distant ancestors saw to that long ago with those ancient fireside tales.

No, the originality comes from what you bring to the table, the perspective you look out on the darkness with, the way you wrestle that fog into a shape no one has ever seen before.

So the next time you're struck with a thought, trying to tackle a concept, or just want to explore your own mind, let yourself. Turn out the lights and go in a direction you never saw coming. Go traveling.

What you find in the dark may surprise you.

A Jaunt/y/ Past Time

A hazelnut scream in a chocolate dream and I realize I'm visiting *abstract* again. A cold wind blows amid the treasure troves, and the fire dragons curling around them tell me dreams of sleep shall never make me weep. The mournful dirge moans low. My mind is constructing a sea chantey and penning it in epic form; I'm not really sure why. Thoughts crystallize and resume lucidity for a transient instant in the fog. It pierces like an ice tower, fac(e)ts blinding in the passing sun.

Why can't we make our language work for us? We get too caught up in one meaning of a word when a word is so many other words clustering together in a nested matryoshka shell of infinitely branching trees; narrowing it down to one bare shaven twig would rob our minds of the very luster of words.

Distinction.

I stare at it in my head and see the countless layers behind the wor(l)d that meld into one amorphous whole. If you could walk ninety degrees around the side of the wor(l)d, you would see it expanded, composed of thin layers, each slice its own definition. Our writing and reading (in three dimensions, these two are layered on top of each other along with logic, reason, way of life, still trapped by linearity even now!, as one simultaneous instant of recognition) are two-dimensional, why can't we add the third? Flat words on flat screens rolling steadily onward, a to b to c; line(a)r; dry.

(I wo/a/nder what you will see in that rulesbound (smashthem) attempt at/to/ ig<n>or/e/ing time)

((Lower down I am even more curious as to which subconscious is responsible for symbol recognition))

(((Can one create a shared meaning if each cypher is unique?)))

((((Is there a balance between one|all?))))

Every word is a painting, an intertwining masterpiece of past present future, yet paintings go for one thousand times the price of words. Richly jeweled treasures valued at monochromatic coals; is it any wonder we don't know how to talk to each other? So [many] trapped by [locked] minds unable to grasp all those glittering facets. So [much] [lost].

My cypher unlocks this p/i<e>a/ce. Will yours?

How to Serve Man

Hello, future alien invader/tyrannical despot/machine overmind. If you're reading this, then no doubt you'd like to know the best way to fatten up humanity for your inevitable consumption of said humanity's delicious meaty bits.

Don't fret! I'm here to help, and it's actually a very simple process.

The first thing you'll want to do is procure a charismatic leader. Human beings love to fall all over themselves abdicating responsibility to someone who has a deep baritone voice, a fancy mustache, or, possibly, a funny hat. Bonus points if the guy has been on television or radio at some point — everyone loves a mass-media personality. The actual issues aren't important; the main thing is that your avatar should look good while discussing them. You see, humanity has a thing for the appearance of something over its actual substance. We humans are crazy for the conniving, suckers for the superficial, devourers of the deceitful. If the outward appearance tells a beautiful story, we don't care what the underlying moral might be. Good, evil, indifferent—it doesn't matter. Give us a sound bite and we're good to go.

Why think about the real when we can make a snap judgment about the illusion?

The second thing you'll want to do is give your figurehead an impressive title—something like king, queen, pope, bishop, general, or president. For whatever reason, humans love to follow someone with a title. It doesn't really matter what that title is, or even if it's legitimate; the important thing is that your stalking horse has some sort of fancy name. Hell, look at all the terrible people throughout human history who have convinced millions to follow them by claiming that some sort of moral authority or power has been conferred on them from an invisible being—it's foolproof! As Living Colour so famously sang, you want a cult of personality. Stalin, Mao, Hitler—exploiters, revered leaders, influencers all, their true selves clearly visible to those who cared to look. Here's a hint: not many cared to look.

The third thing, and this is very important, is to make sure your figurehead is always consistent in his beliefs, no matter how asinine those beliefs may be. He insists that the world was created seven thousand years ago and disregards the massive amount of physical evidence suggesting that's not the case? Not a problem. He states that other races are less than human because their skin is a particular color in the visible spectrum? Don't even worry about it. He declares that crazy alien overlords live in a volcano and the only way to escape them is to donate more and more money to the person in charge? As long as your candidate sticks to his guns, people won't give a single fuck.

You see, it's not about whether your figurehead is right or wrong; it's about how much he *believes*. As long as he *believes* in something 100 percent, it doesn't matter if the facts match reality. All people care about is if he is all in, if he's dedicated himself entirely to an ideal, no matter how outlandish, no matter how ludicrous, no matter how idiotic. All they want is someone who can stand in front of a thousand cameras and say, "This is the truth as I see it," even if that person is absolutely irrational and self-destructive. They want to know that they aren't alone in their stupidity, that someone else shares their neuroses and flaws. They want the comfort of the herd.

The wonderful thing about humanity, the absolutely glorious fact that no one seems to know, is that humanity wants to serve. People want to obey. They don't want to look at the hard questions in life and try to figure out answers.

No, human beings want someone to tell them what to do. They want direction, guidance, a master.

Humanity is lazy. Human beings want a savior to tell them, "This is right, and this is wrong. This is grace, and this is sin. This is Heaven, and this is Hell." They want a leader to shout, "The Jews are evil—throw them in a furnace and strike the match." They want a prophet to declare, "Women are unclean, cover them lest you be tempted to sin, and deny them their freedom lest they tempt you to damnation." They need a leader to shine a light on their darkest desires and their secret hopes and tell them that it's okay to indulge in their hate, and then, oh boy, will they ever indulge.

Are you that leader? If you can provide a path, a blueprint, a way to realize that intolerance, then humans will follow you into whatever oven you want to roast them in (preferably with a sprig of parsley and just a hint of garlic butter). A sheep doesn't question where the herd is taking it, it just follows in contentment, baaing all the way off the cliff. A sheep wants the blind certitude of certainty, the dull comfort of routine, the unthinking small-mindedness of similarity. A sheep is a simple beast and doesn't care to think past the next meal and where it will lie down to sleep.

A sheep wants a shepherd, and that's what you have to provide—a crook to guide the herd, a staff to beat the wayward back in line, a strong voice the meek will obey without question. If you want to serve man, search for his deepest desires, his basest motivations, his willingness to subsume himself in an idea that will never be in his best interests, and then give him someone to follow.

He'll thank you all the way into your stomach.

Bang Bang

WARNING: THERE ARE NAUGHTY WORDS IN THIS AND IF THAT OFFENDS YOU, TOUGH SHIT.

Dear Second Amendment Gun Nuts,

I'm sick and tired of you guys being assholes. Gun violence in the United States continues to increase (I'm writing this on the day of the Newtown, Connecticut, shooting), and the only thing you self-righteous fucks want to do is piss and moan about how your precious right to carry a death machine is being taken away from you.

Stop it.

Seriously, stop it. I understand that guns are tools, and that a gun requires a human being to pull the trigger, but every time one of these tragedies occurs, we as a nation are prevented from having any sort of meaningful dialogue about it because cum-gargling shitmilitias immediately start attacking anyone who even hints that stricter gun control might not be such a bad idea. *"ERMAGERD, IF THEY TAKE ERR GUNZ WE CAN'T FIGHT THE FEDARALIS WHEN THEY INVADE THE COMPOUND!! SLIPPERY SLOPE!! SECOND 'MEND-MENT!! SECOND 'MENDMENT!!"*

Listen up, fuckwits. The Second Amendment is absogoddamn-lutely worthless in this day and age. If the government ever wanted to seriously oppress you, IT HAS TANKS AND AIR-PLANES. Your kitted-out AR-15 with folding bipod, bitchin' thermal scope, and custom-engraved Dale Earnhardt bald eagle on the grip will do approximately jack *and* shit to any sort of modern mechanized force, especially one operating within its own logistical-supply theater. The only thing your gun is good for is killing someone who *isn't* from the govern-ment, and citizens having guns so they can kill people who aren't from the government is pretty much exactly the opposite of what the Second Amendment is for.

Pop quiz number one: Do you know what the tech level was when our Founding Fathers wrote the Second Amendment? Single-shot muskets. The Second Amendment guaranteed citi-zens the right to bear arms because they could *effectively* hold their own against an oppressive government force. Both sides would be equipped with the same weaponry, and a well-armed citizen militia would actually stand a fighting chance of defeat-ing a power-hungry president or rogue federal agency.

Pop quiz number two: Do you know what you need to blow up a mainline M1A1 Abrams battle tank? SOMETHING LARGER THAN A FUCKING GLOCK, YOU STUPID MOUTH-BREATHER. There's no longer parity between the amount of force available to a citizen of the United States and the amount of force at the disposal of the United States government. If the government seriously wants to oppress you, it's going to fucking oppress you. Bend over, spread your ass cheeks, and try not to cry too much. The drones will be recording it all, and you don't want to embarrass yourself.

Pop quiz number three: If a SWAT team hits the wrong house (which has happened multiple times) and kicks open your door in the middle of the night, how friendly will these men be when they see you pointing something threatening at them? Do not try to kill the SWAT team. That's absolutely asinine. The solution is better police oversight and education, not a Bushmaster with armor-piercing rounds; if you try that, you'll find out firsthand what "You'll get my gun when you pry it from my cold, dead fingers" actually means.

So let's call it like it is. No more hiding behind "Well, if the government takes our guns, how can we prevent the tyrants from taking over?" The tyrants are already in control, and they have been for a while. No, the reason you want to keep flooding the streets with easily accessible guns is that you're too fucking lazy to think for yourselves. You'd rather buy into the NRA propaganda machine and spin yourself a nice little fantasy, one where you single-handedly defeat the dastardly hordes of black-suited, sunglasses-wearing federal soul snatchers who come to tell you freedom ain't ringin' no more and yet somehow avoid any repercussions from committing multiple homicides. Or perhaps, in your fantasy, you're living the James Bond life, sipping a martini while a supermodel hangs off your arm and strokes your engorged nine-millimeter.

Pop quiz number four: Any idea who funds the NRA? PEOPLE WHO MAKE MONEY FROM SELLING GUNS. Seriously—go look it up, it's right on the NRA Web site.

Imagine that. A group of businesses that have vested interests in seeing that guns are easily available for people to buy supporting an organization that pushes legislation to make guns easier to buy. Despite the fact that, you know, their product is used to kill people, and *has* been used to kill people—over, and over, and over. Details, details, the devil's always in the details.

Speaking of details, here's an interesting one: Despite the proliferation of concealed-carry laws and the loosening of gun restrictions, in the past thirty years, not a single mass shooting has been stopped by a civilian carrying a gun (http://www .motherjones.com/politics/2012/07/mass-shootings-map). Shootings have been stopped by police officers or by the offenders suiciding, but there is not a single instance of an armed civilian putting a stop to a rampage.

Yeah, that whole bit about "If only more people carried guns, none of this would be happening"? Total bullshit. Guess who wants you to carry more guns. The people who make more guns. I wonder what possible motive they could have.

Oh, wait—I figured it out. They want to make money, and they don't really give a fuck if people die because of it.

To be fair to the Gun Nuts, though, our problem isn't strictly the proliferation of firearms in America (though that's a big part of it, and we need better control over our weapons). The problem, ladies and gentlemen, is us.

As a society, we glorify gun violence in everything from movies to books to video games to television shows. We sexy it up with action scenes and history specials; we celebrate it in first-person shooters and war games; we sanitize it by not showing the consequences of what happens to a human being when a gun is used against him. Don't show any blood, heaven forbid the children see some blood, but so long as everyone dies off-screen, you can kill as many hapless extras as you want, guns blazing the entire time. Gotta make sure you get that PG-13 rating so as many impressionable adolescents as possible can drive up your box-office revenues.

(Personal note: That last paragraph was difficult for me to write. Everyone who knows me knows I love to play video games, and I also enjoy playing first-person shooters. However, to deny the fact that they highlight an underlying problem in our society is willful blindness, and I try not to knowingly lie to myself. Honestly, we should use these games to teach consequences to our children—if you die in an FPS, that shit needs to carry some weight. Instead of you re-spawning, perhaps your console gets bricked and all your gamer-score achieve-points are deleted, or maybe you have to donate one hundred dollars to mental-health care and veteran services every time you reload. If you want to play with guns, there's always a cost. Probably going to be tough to get that one by marketing, though. I mean, who would want to play something that had real consequences attached to losing?

Also, parents, pay some fucking attention to what your children are playing/watching/reading. You should not be letting an eight-year-old play a mature-rated game or watch *Sons of Anarchy*. Show some common sense, and actually invest something in your kid. It'll pay off in the long run. Back on topic.)

As a society, we see mental illness as a stigma, not a disease to be treated. We build prisons instead of hospitals, and then we wonder why someone who's "not right in the head" does something crazy instead of getting help. We see going to therapy and counseling as signs of weakness, not as an attempt to heal a sick body part. How fucking ridiculous would it be if someone made fun of you for doing physical rehab after a knee surgery? "Ha-ha, you stupid jerk, you're so weak. Real men just walk off their ACL tears."

Idiotic. Yet that's what we do! We continue to cut funding for health care, especially for mental-health issues, and we treat our mentally ill like rabid animals. We force them to live on the street, or we lock them in prison and give them no assistance, but if they want to buy a gun, it's no questions asked, make sure you get some bullets in aisle four.

So, Gun Nuts, please, if nothing else sways you, at least think on this: Is your gun really that important to you? Is it worth another classroom of dead children? Is it worth teenagers solving their problems with bullets instead of words, cutting off forever the possibilities of life? Is it worth denying American citizens the opportunity to have a meaningful conversation just because you'd rather support some corporation's bottom line instead of basic human dignity and empathy?

We are killing ourselves, we are killing our neighbors, and we are killing our children, all in the name of greed and power. We can be better than this. We have to be better than this, because if we're not, we're murdering our future.

Bang bang.

Sincerely,

Someone Who Has Shot Several Guns, Enjoys Playing Shooting Games, Knows Your Slippery Slope Argument Is Utter Tripe, and Realizes Enough Is Fucking Enough

Thirty Pieces

I've been struggling with how to write this piece for a while now, because it is simultaneously very simple and very complex. Here's the simple part:

Our currency, and, by extension, our society, in its present state is worthless.

The complex part is how to explain it.

Money is a representation. In and of itself, it has minimal value (you can burn the bills for warmth, but that's about it). We used to peg money to an arbitrary gold standard, but that's fool's gold (all it takes is one captured metal-rich asteroid to shatter that bubble). What money represents, what all currencies ultimately represent, is time. There are always going to be about twenty-four hours in the day here on Earth (yay leap seconds), and everyone has an equal amount of time each day that he or she is alive.

When you exchange money for a good or service, you're

trading the time you spent doing whatever job it is that you do for the time the people you're paying spent doing whatever it is that they do. Society places a value on how much your time is worth in relation to what you produce. Let's look at how we value time in this country. (If you want to find these numbers, just Google *median [job] compensation*. The numbers are the closest approximations I could find; I use median because average tends to skew the numbers higher. The numbers will likely have changed from the time I wrote this piece, and I'm betting they're not closer together.)

Median CEO salary — $9.6 million
Median NBA player salary — $2.33 million
Median NFL player salary — $770,000
Median physician salary — $278,000 (figures vary with specialties)
Median farmer/rancher salary — $60,000
Median teacher salary — $55,000
Median firefighter salary — $42,000
Median janitor salary — $22,000

So what do these numbers tell us? That for every one year a CEO works, a doctor has to work around 34, a teacher or farmer or firefighter has to work around 175, and a janitor has to work around 436.

This is ridiculous. We value the people who keep us healthy, fed, and educated far less than those who tell others what to do or those who play children's games. You're telling me that one year of my life spent kicking a football (I make a bit above the median) is worth almost four years of a doctor's services? That what I do on a football field is more important than twenty-two years of teaching classrooms of children? That someone can spend six lifetimes cleaning up after people and preventing the spread of germs and disease and still barely approach a year's worth of shuffling stock portfolios and mergers, of making conference calls and speculating (wildly at times) on bonds and futures?

I say no. While I spend a lot of time honing my craft, there is absolutely no way what I do even comes close to benefiting society as much as the work of a doctor or a teacher or a janitor. I clean no floors; I cure no sick; I put out no fires. But society continues to pay me and people like me obscene amounts of money. People give us their time! They're telling companies and con men, "We would rather be entertained and distracted than focus on building a better future. We would rather elect politicians who pass morality laws and tax cuts to help the rich get richer and vote for a quick fix that makes us feel good now than address the root problems of our system."

That is why our money is worthless. We value the short term, the shallow, the parasitic leeches of society more than those who actually contribute to long-term stability and growth. We value time spent obfuscating and concealing more than time spent creating and teaching. And what's worse is that we've made it a given in politics that only those who can afford to play get to run. Want to hold office? Better get that money for radio and television ads.

We've created a feedback loop that inevitably spirals down into oppression and decay, as those with money become ever more concerned with getting more money, more power, more control over laws and regulations until the whole house of cards comes crashing down. Take a look at the current election cycle, at the voter-ID amendments and bills being proposed, at the efforts to gradually narrow the vote down to those who have cash. As someone who has studied history, I can tell you that every time a society places short-term gains over long-term stability, turns exclusive instead of inclusive, and resorts to petty factionalism and bickering (in this society, that means arguing over who deserves to be called a "real 'Murrican")—well, let's just say it doesn't end well.

PS: Some may call me a hypocrite for being a part of the system, for entertaining rather than teaching. To you I say this: Change the system. Put me out of a job. Pay the teachers and firefighters and doctors and janitors what you pay me, and I'll gladly do those jobs instead. Value the useful and not the merely entertaining or self-promoting; give a voice to the currently voiceless. Unfortunately, as it stands, I can operate only in the framework we've all created, the society that millions upon millions of Americans erect every Sunday, every election cycle, with every bailed-out bank and golden parachute funded while bridges crumble and schools shut down.

Are you not entertained?

For the Children

If there's one thing I've noticed over the years, it's that people love to use the "it's for the children" argument whenever they feel like they're on shaky logical ground. I've seen it used in arguments against teaching evolution in schools and against gun control (/boggle), but nowhere have I seen it used more vociferously and alarmingly than in the fight against same-sex marriage.

"If the gays start getting married, how am I supposed to explain that to my children?! What do I say when two men or women walk down the street holding hands?! My children are going to be so confused by this behavior that there's a one hundred percent chance they'll turn gay! WON'T SOMEBODY THINK OF THE CHILDREN?!?!"

Unfortunately, what every single one of these shrieking harpies fails to realize is that they're not, in fact, thinking of the children when they start spewing their ignorance. They're thinking of themselves. They're thinking of their own inability to accept the fact that two people of the same sex might happen to love each other, but they have an inkling that if they say they can't accept it, they're going to be called bigots, so they mask their fear and stupidity with the strongest shield they can think of.

The children.

Well, I, for one, am tired of seeing children used to disguise bigotry. I'm tired of watching the "morally upright" teach generation after generation that it's okay to preach vitriol and obscenity as long as you include the phrase "for the children." Above all, I'm tired of all those people who don't have the courage to face what's in their own hearts and then work to change for the better, to be inclusive rather than exclusive.

That's why I wrote my letter to Delegate Burns. That's why I go on interviews and do podcasts, and that's why I'm writing this book.

Because it IS about the children. It's just not about the children in the way some people think.

It's about homosexual parents having recourse to the same laws and access to the same benefits, the same protections, that every other heterosexual parent has access to so their children can have the same advantages and chances to succeed in life. It's about a child not having to worry about being bullied at school or on the street because she happens to be different. It's about a child being able to live in a stable home with parents who love each other and who just so happen to be the same sex, because every scientific study done shows no disadvantage or harm in being raised by gay parents.

It's about giving our children the tools to succeed in life—tools like empathy and kindness. It's about creating a nurturing environment so our children can grow up to be whoever they want to be and not face any stigma for their choices. It's about understanding that there are countless children and they're not all going to be the same and that we should celebrate that diversity as they mature into adults.

It's also about the world our children are going to live in and the attitudes of the people in it. Will our children grow up with tolerance and respect, treating others the way they'd like to be treated? Or will they grow up with discrimination and hate, divided from those around them, subject to the same stupid cycle of anger and strife, the same racism and sexism we've overcome before? Will they live in peace? Or will they be subject to rage and pain, the violence of the mob ever present?

So please, think of the children, but with love, not fear.

Graduation

Well, this is awkward. I'm not one for graduation speeches, frankly, because I think most of them are a waste of perfectly good time that could be spent reading or doing something useful, and now I've been asked to write one. I mean, what are you supposed to tell a group of students who are getting ready to head out into the big wide world? How do you make them understand that their entire school life has been about teaching them things they didn't know they were learning?

Let's be honest here—90 percent of the crap you learn in school is useless out in the real world. Will you ever need to know who Archduke Franz Ferdinand was in any rational social setting? No, you won't (he was the ostensible trigger for World War I, if you're curious). Will you ever be asked to find the cosine of an isosceles triangle at a dinner party? *Nyet* (unless you hang out with some really weird people, or mathematicians). The presumptive eating habits of the northern European aurochs? Seriously. Just no.

All the little facts, all the trivia, all the dates and places and names are not the reason you're graduating. Everything you need to know to function in your job, you'll learn at your job. Sure, there's some general knowledge you've hopefully picked up— how to add and subtract so you don't get shortchanged at the grocery store; the cardinal directions of a compass in case you get lost; that you shouldn't piss upstream of where you get your drinking water—but, really, that's applicable no matter what you choose to do.

No, the reason you're graduating is that (hopefully) you've learned how to interact with other people, how to navigate social situations, and how to master new information, no matter what it might be. The world is made up of all sorts of different people, and it doesn't matter what grades any of you got, what classes you took, if you didn't learn the most important lesson of all.

People are complex. People are incredibly kind and amazingly selfish. People are altruistic angels and conniving sociopaths. People are smart, stupid, wise, foolish, funny, boring, and so many other things it would take me all day to list them. People were at the parties you went to, throwing up on the balcony, dancing on the tables, making questionable decisions, having a good time, and creepily eyeing the pretty girls (or pretty boys, whatever makes them happy).

Every conversation you had over a beer, or in your dorm room, or during class; every interaction with anyone you ever met was a lesson about the real world and what you'll find in it. That asshole professor who said your work wasn't good enough and who gave you lower grades than you deserved? Yeah, you'll meet him again in life. He'll probably be your boss, and he'll be just as much of a dick.

Side note: If any of you professors out there realize that this applies to you, stop being such a dick. Seriously. I know you have to deal with a lot of students, but remember that your behavior influences them just as much as your subject matter does. You're role models for children who will one day be role models for other children, and the lessons you pass down will continue long after you're gone.

Back to the students. The classes you took—not important. What's important is that you learned *how* to learn during those classes, how to distill information from a variety of sources to get at the small nuggets of truth hidden within. Don't just blindly follow whatever a book says; examine who wrote it and what her agenda might have been, what biases she may have brought with her. Logic and reason are your friends, and if you can't logically connect the dots in an argument, ANY argument, then your opinion is not worth listening to. I can't tell you how many times I've had conversations with people who base their arguments on "Because I think that's the way it is" or "Because that's the way it's always been done," or how many times I've heard people cite statistics without knowing what they actually mean or how they were acquired. These people never learned how to *learn*—they learned how to parrot. Please, don't be a parrot.

Question everything, but don't do it just for the sake of being contrary (though that can be fun at times). Question when the stats don't line up with the conclusion being drawn, question when the ethical implications are clearly wrong, question whenever you think someone is trying to hide something or pass a lie off as the truth, because *that's* what you should have been learning. How to think for yourself. How not to be a slave to someone else's unthinking dogma. How to live your own life.

So go forth and live your own life. Whatever you choose to do, do it to the best of your ability, but never forget the people around you, the people you interact with. Our world is only as good as we're willing to make it, and that means treating others how we want to be treated, letting others live in freedom so they'll let us do the same. No matter how much or how little money you make, how successful (or not) your career is, all we have is each other.

All we have are the people we spend our lives with.

Good luck.

All Your Bases

The core of a stable society is a tripod, the legs of which are the following:

Empathy—Without its people possessing a fully developed
sense of empathy, a society has no freedom. It is only through
accepting the differences of others that a stable polity can
develop, and any attempt to marginalize or discriminate
against minority groups will lead to conflict farther down
the road as they agitate for equality wrongfully denied them.

Logic—The ability to reason and make decisions free of fear
and ignorance is the only way to create beneficial long-
term growth in a society. Coupled with empathy, logic
allows individuals to make altruistic choices that benefit
the many over the few by promoting an atmosphere of

equality—as life gets better for everyone, opportunities for conflict diminish.

Enlightened Self-Interest—The drive to constantly improve, but not at the cost of long-term harm to the society, is the core of enlightened self-interest. Combined with logic, this leads to the understanding that short-term gains are never prioritized over long-term consequences; the citizens understand that the society will endure after an individual passes on. Coupled with empathy, enlightened self-interest will never cost another individual his rights, as that leads inevitably to conflict.

The rights of individuals in a stable society are:

The Right to Free Will—Whatever actions consenting adults take that do not deprive other individuals of the opportunity to exercise their own free will are nobody's goddamned business but the people's involved. Live your own life and let other people live theirs.

The Right to Knowledge—All individuals must have access to the fundamental basics of education and all information available in the society. The only way for a person to make rational choices is to have all the information in hand so he can weigh the potential benefits and consequences. Ignorance can be only a personal choice, not the enforcement of others. All requests for information will themselves be a matter of public record; a truly free society has no need for privacy laws because everyone knows who is watching at any given time.

The Right to Humanity — Any individual, regardless of race, gender, species, or origin (biological or nonbiological), who can demonstrate empathy, logic, and enlightened self-interest shall be regarded as human and benefit from all rights and protections afforded thereof. Appearances don't mean a thing. Actions do.

Who Is John Galt?

So I forced myself to read *Atlas Shrugged*. Apparently I harbor masochistic tendencies; it was a long, hard slog, and by the end I felt as if Ayn Rand had violently beaten me about the head and shoulders with words. I feel I would be doing all of you a disservice (especially those who think Rand is really super-duper awesome) if I didn't share some thoughts on this weighty tome.

Who is John Galt?

John Galt (as written in said novel) is a deeply flawed, sociopathic ideal of the perfect human. John Galt does not recognize the societal structure surrounding him that allows him to exist. John Galt, to be frank, is a turd.

However, John Galt is also very close to greatness. The only thing he is missing, the only thing Ayn Rand forgot to take into account when writing *Atlas Shrugged,* is empathy.

John Galt talks about intelligence and education without

discussing who will pay for the schools, who will teach the teachers. John Galt has no thought for his children, or their children, or what kind of world they will have to occupy when the mines run out and the streams dry up. John Galt expects an army to protect him but has no concern about how it's funded or staffed. John Galt spends his time in a valley where no disasters occur, no accidents happen, and no real life takes place.

John Galt lives in a giant fantasy that's no different from an idealistic communist paradise or an anarchist's playground or a capitalist utopia. His world is flat and two-dimensional. His world is not real, and that is the huge, glaring flaw with objectivism.

John Galt does not live in reality.

In reality, hurricanes hit coastlines, earthquakes knock down buildings, people crash cars or trip over rocks or get sick and miss work. In reality, humans make good choices and bad choices based on forces even they sometimes don't understand. To live with other human beings, to live in society, requires that we understand that shit happens and sometimes people need a safety net. Empathy teaches us that contributing to this safety net is beneficial for all, because we never know when it will be our turn.

If an earthquake destroys half the merchandise in my store or levels my house, that's something I can't control; it doesn't matter how prepared I was or how hard I worked. Trying to recover from something like that can cripple a person, both financially and mentally, unless he has some help from those who understand that we're all in this together, we need each other to function as a society, and the next earthquake might hit one of *our* houses.

If a volcano erupts and takes out vital transportation and infrastructure, should we just throw our hands up in the air and say, "Not my responsibility"? No, because it *is* our responsibility.

It's our responsibility as members of a societal group to take care of the underlying foundations of peace and security—to ensure that the roads and rails are protected because they provide a collective good.

To be fair to John Galt, though, the safety net cannot be a security blanket. If you hand one person everything in life by taking it away from someone else, then the will to succeed rapidly fades on both sides; why work when it doesn't matter? Look at any of the idle rich, the spoiled children of privilege, the welfare collectors who churn out babies because it means another weekly check to buy shoes or purses. Ayn Rand got it right up to that point but fails to make the next logical step.

If you want to get rid of the moocher, you don't do it by excluding everyone you think could be a moocher, by building your own private jail with yourself as both warden and prisoner. No, if you want to rid yourself of the moocher, you do it by focusing on and teaching rational empathy. If you treat other people the way you want to be treated, you'll never want someone else to live your life for you, because shackling others means you've chosen to shackle yourself. We're all free, or we're all slaves.

No one wants to take care of someone who does nothing in return, provides no value for society (I'm ignoring babies and children here, because they're kind of necessary to the long-term survival of humanity), and so the corollary applies—if you feel that everyone should be free to live his or her own life, the safety net can never become a permanent solution, because if you rely overmuch on it, then you're no longer living your own life.

Just as you don't want other people to be an unnecessary burden on you, you should desire just as much not to be an unnecessary burden on others. If you take handouts when you no longer need them, you've turned yourself into a slave to someone else. If you think that other people have to take care of you but that you don't have to take care of them in return, you're trying to enslave those who would provide for you. If you make people dependent on you by limiting their opportunities for education and work and requiring them to subsist on a dole, you've taken away their chance at free will, at making their own lives.

John Galt as written lacks this rational empathy. John Galt is brilliant but doesn't have the long-term vision to maintain the society that allowed his brilliance to flourish. John Galt is self-motivated but has no concern for the effects of his actions on other people. John Galt is a lone individual living in a world filled with countless teeming masses, and just as John Galt plants his feet on the backs of all those who came before him, he must provide a surface for future generations to plant their feet as well, not through sacrificing everything he owns but by realizing a stable society is ultimately a productive society.

But that's not John Galt. A world full of Ayn Rand's John Galts is a world that will eventually consist of only one person, and then none, once his lifespan concludes. John Galt doesn't care for the disasters that affect his neighbors — they can sink or swim on their own (and they'll sink). John Galt doesn't care for the public good, because all he can see is his own good (and he'll wonder why it gets harder and harder to get the resources he needs). John Galt doesn't recognize that genius arises under any circumstances (and he'll never know how many geniuses he excluded from paradise because their parents didn't fit his ideals, or why the population keeps shrinking).

John Galt is a remorseless shark feeding on those unable to get out of his way, the blood-churned waters boiling around him as he takes in everything he requires for his own happiness without thought of the cost to others, rending and tearing the stability of social interactions until his once-teeming world is barren and life-less, collapsed under the gluttonous appetite of self.

Then he starves, and no one is left to mourn his passing.

Are you John Galt?

Incorporation

I've been doing some serious thinking lately, and I've decided I'm going to take the plunge. There's no reason not to — the benefits are quite substantial, and there's really no downside to doing it. Frankly, the more time I spend in the modern world, the more surprised I am that someone hasn't figured it out earlier.

I'm talking, obviously, of registering my body as a corporation, with my mind as a limited liability representative.

All the important components are already in place, so really all that's left is the paperwork. I have a board of directors (they're quite argumentative at times, especially when Rationality and Emotion start going at it, or when Primal Urge feels unfulfilled), and they all have local addresses and can be easily contacted (except when they don't feel like it). I've issued stock to various outside investors, letting them dictate how much value they own (because money, after all, is merely the abstraction of time spent performing a task). My wife and football are the majority owners right now, but the kids are starting an aggressive buyout, and I think in a couple years they'll have almost full control. There's also a list of corporate bylaws that I made up myself and follow when it doesn't inconvenience me, so I don't foresee any legal holdup.

Once I register, I think the benefits are really going to be worth it. My taxes will be much lower than they are now, so that'll definitely go over well with the shareholders, and having limited liability will make certain functions of life a lot easier. If I ever kill someone, or steal a bunch of money, or bribe people to get a more favorable outcome on something I want, I'll just pay a small fine and not even have to say I did anything wrong. It's awesome! I couldn't even be charged with a serious crime, unlike you silly normal people. I could literally walk down to the local Federal Reserve and take a couple billion dollars, and as long as I paid back several million and promised never to do it again (not that I did anything wrong in the first place, of course), there'd be no problem whatsoever. Everyone's a winner!

(By *everyone*, I obviously mean "my board of directors," because that's all that really matters. Why should I care how other people are affected by my body's actions? Not liable, remember?)

There's also the environmental aspect to think of. Once I declare my body a corporation, it's not my fault if what I do harms the world around me. I have to look out for my shareholders, so if that means I run over a couple pedestrians to get to work faster or throw a bunch of dirty diapers in my neighbor's backyard rather than take the time to go put it in the trash, they can rest assured that I'm working for their best interests. The more time I spend with them, the more value they get, and, frankly, that's the only guideline I have to follow.

You can be damned sure I'll be talking to policy crafters accordingly. Luckily, I'll be able to use as much money as I want to influence their decisions about what to set into law, so, thanks, Supreme Court! Thanks, Washington! Appreciate the assist!

Now, don't get me wrong, there *are* a couple downsides. First off, to get that preferred tax rate, I'm going to have to base my corporation in the Cayman Islands or some other business-friendly nation, so that'll necessitate a couple copies of myself to act as shell companies. They don't really have to do anything, just sit there and provide the polite legal fiction that I'm actually residing in that country, so I'll probably just get a couple of Fatheads or something and glue them to the side of a local strip mall. They won't even need to pick up the phone if someone calls (which is a good thing, since inanimate objects traditionally struggle with phone-answering etiquette), but those shipping costs are going to set me back at least twenty or thirty bucks. Hopefully I'll save that much with the tax laws.

Second, I can't do anything totally shocking or horrendous until I'm so big that everyone in the world would be devastated by the mere thought of losing me.

Obviously, I'll need to start a reality-television show or something similar to ensure that everyone who has time invested in me will be completely unable to function in any way, shape, or form if I disappear. Even the possibility of not having me around should be enough to drive the world into such a panic that otherwise completely rational people will mortgage away their future for the totally essential services I provide (chiefly: being me), but the only way to make this happen is for me to repeatedly tell people just how necessary I am to their well-being. Remember: You need me. I complete you. If I'm not here, your life is meaningless, and you'll probably end up starving in a gutter somewhere. I can't really prove this in any substantial way, but I know *I'll* be adversely affected if I'm dissolved or broken up, so just trust me on this one. I've repeated myself so many times, there's no chance it's a lie.

Finally, I'm not sure how I'm going to deal with the perpetuation of my corporation once those on the current board of directors decide to call it quits, but to be honest, I've offered them some pretty big bonuses to stick around for as long as possible (no matter how they perform), so I'm not too concerned. There's no way my board would ever do anything not in the best interests of the corporation and purely for its own selfish benefit, so once I finish my seventh shot of tequila and do this line of blow, I'm going to drive on down to the local chamber of commerce and get the ball rolling.

It's time to start living life the way it was meant to be lived— as a soulless conglomerate of ideas and desires whose only concern is to make as much profit as possible regardless of harm inflicted on those surrounding it.

It's time to incorporate.

Elementary

Today I had the most intriguing case. It all started when a rather portly gentleman entered my office after hesitantly pushing the glass-paneled door aside. Sweat stains marred the underarms of a wrinkled three-piece suit while his hands nervously clutched at each other like writhing snakes. The top of his scalp glistened in the overhead light, and a thinning fringe of hair ran around it like a monk's tonsure—referred to in current street slang as a Republican mohawk, I believe. He smelled vaguely of hemp and whiskey.

I leaned back in my chair and crossed one foot over the other atop my battered desk, carefully avoiding kicking my laptop onto the thinly carpeted floor, and waited for whatever it was he had to say.

"Sir," he began, tremulously, "I wish to hire you to find something for me, something that I appear to have mislaid. Countless groups claimed they could help, but they all contradicted each other, and, frankly, I'm in such a deplorable state now that I've nowhere else to turn. I heard about your skills of deductive reasoning from the Internet pages, heard about your reputation for honesty and forthrightness. I'm desperate at this point, sir, and you appear to be the last option available to me. You have no idea how hard it is to find an honest man these days . . ."

He trailed off into silence, head down, eyes staring vacantly at the floor. His hands had grown still throughout the impassioned plea and now hung loosely at his sides. In all respects, a picture of utter and abject despair.

"Why should I help you?" I asked him bluntly. I do not suffer fools gladly, and his foolishness was beginning to irritate me. "What reason is there for me not to simply tell you to be on your way, along with your obsequious whining?"

"Why, sir, because it is the decent thing to do!" He drew back, affronted. "Do you feel no moral obligation to help those in need? Have you no charitable instinct toward those less fortunate than yourself?"

"I do," I replied, "but that still doesn't answer my question. You said you needed my help finding something you misplaced, yet if you but simply retrace your steps, you shall be sure to find it. Tell me again: Why should I help you when I do not feel particularly inclined to do so?"

"Well, I can pay you, pay you vast sums of money; you'll have more wealth than you could ever imagine." He squinted narrowly as he peered at me. "I happen to be one of the wealthiest people in the world, and I'm sure I could make some of that lucre trickle down into your coffers."

I laughed. "Nonsense. You don't have an actual penny to your name. Try a different tack."

His face grew flushed as he clenched his fists. "How dare you say that to me, you insolent little brat!" he bellowed. "Where do you get off making such a preposterous claim?"

I raised a hand and began ticking points off on my fingers. "One: Your suit. It's of a fine make, but that style hasn't been worn in at least fifteen years, which means it's from either the back of your closet or a thrift store. It hangs comfortably on the shoulders and neck, which rules out thrift store, but it's a little tight around the waist, which tells me you got it when you were younger. It was probably a celebratory outfit, based on that particular cut, which is too formal for everyday wear. You've worn it often since then, as the shinier patches on the elbows and knees attest, but not recently, which I deduce from the unmistakable aroma of mothballs that even now hangs in the air, and since my office is definitely not the site of a debutante's ball or any other celebration, that means you've pawned off everything else of value that could possibly impress someone.

"Two: Your fingernails are scuffed and dirty and your hair is oily, though neatly combed around the edges in an attempt to hide that fact. The comb itself is a cheap plastic version, the end of which I can see barely sticking out of your right pocket, and multiple teeth are missing. A fastidious man, one who aligns both shirtsleeves to be geometrically precise with his jacket, would keep his hands and hair clean unless he had no other option, and he would replace such a comb at the earliest possible opportunity. The fact you are unable to do so suggests a severe lack of funds, as well as a lack of access to common utilities.

"Three: I can see the outline of several coins and crumpled banknotes in your left trouser pocket but no wallet bulge anywhere, which tells me that you're running on empty. A wealthy man wouldn't bother with the coins and wouldn't be without access to at least some of his wealth at a moment's notice, especially if he was planning on using that wealth. You've tracked in some oil on the bottom of your shoe, yet I don't hear any keys jingling when you walk, which means you didn't pick up the oil when you were in a gas station filling up your car; you got it while asking for the change that I mentioned earlier. Except I don't think you asked for the change, because that brings me to point four.

"Point four is the revolver sitting in a shoulder holster underneath your left arm. The sweat pattern is distributed in the silhouette of a .356 Magnum, and the powder burns peppering your right hand tell me you've used it recently. Your demeanor and appearance don't indicate any signs of a mugging or other attack, so you must have been the aggressor, and your nonchalant attitude means it's not a new behavior. Hopefully, for your sake, you didn't actually use the gun on somebody today."

I clasped my hands behind my head and continued staring into his now beady eyes. "That is where I 'get off,' as you so eloquently put it. You've neither the intention to pay me nor the means to do so. Now, I'll repeat the question one more time: Why should I help you?"

He grinned unpleasantly, drew the revolver, held it waist high, and aimed it at my head. "Because if you don't, I'll shoot you."

"Ahh, I see, so now we get to the heart of the matter. Very well, if that is your price, let us see if I can pay it. Tell me, what is it that you're looking for?" I swung my feet down and leaned forward, propping my elbows on the desk while steepling my fingers together under my chin.

He took a step toward me, gun still aimed at my temple, and began to speak. "I've lost my way," he stated simply, flatly, angrily.

"I used to have the finest houses, the most expensive cars, piles of money, and I can't find them anymore! They're all in the hands of foreigners and merchants, taken from under my nose! My family was industrious and hardworking, but now all they do is lie about all day complaining that I'm not providing enough for them—as if I have any choice in the matter! That's why I had to shoot that poor towelhead! It was for my family! I keep giving them more and more and it's never enough!"

I sighed and shook my head. "I think I begin to see the problem here. All of your misfortune, all of your complaints, they're all things someone has perpetrated on you, correct?"

He nodded emphatically, lips pursed together in a thin line.

"Well, it seems that we need to discover whoever this person is, and then we shall have an idea as to how we can recover your well-being. Tell me, why does your family no longer work to provide for themselves?"

"I told you, they can't work! All the jobs have been taken by the foreigners! No one wants to pay a decent wage anymore for an honest day's work plus benefits!"

"Surely they must eat, though, correct? Do they grow their own food? Craft their own clothes?"

"Of course not!" He looked shocked. "What do you take us for, savages? There's a wonderful store we use called Mal-Wart, carries everything we need at the only prices we can afford. I tell you, it's an absolute lifesaver. Without those low, low deals, there's no way we'd be able to get by."

"I see. And how do they pay for these wonderful deals?"

"Well, I give my family money, obviously, though it's getting harder and harder to find. Most of what I have goes to supply this beautiful girl." He patted the revolver lovingly. "I don't know what I'd do without her."

"I meant how does *the store* pay for the deals."

"Oh. Well, um, I guess I never thought about it. That's a good question."

I permitted myself a small eye roll while his attention was distracted. "Never mind, never mind, let's move on. Now, you said that merchants were also to blame, is this correct?"

"Yes, that's right!" His voice rose in excitement. "I bet it was one of them what took my fortune, turned it to their own scheming means!" He leaned forward conspiratorially. "A lot of companies are run by those Jews, you know."

"Right. Questions of ownership aside, how, exactly, did these merchants steal from you?"

"Hmm. I couldn't really point to any particulars, but I know they did it somehow." He frowned. "They all needed so much help—to make sure their businesses were established; develop new products, land, and resources for exploitation—so of course I gave it to them. They promised me so much in return, you see, and for a while, I got a little back, and life was good, but then all of a sudden, they said they didn't have any money and couldn't afford to pay me anymore."

"And you believed them?"

"They *were* very convincing. They're the experts, after all; why should I doubt what they tell me? You should see their office buildings—there's no way an idiot would be able to afford something like that. No, these gentlemen are much more intelligent on these affairs than we'll ever be, trust me. If they say they don't have any money, they don't."

"Did they do anything illegal? Fraud? Murder?"

"Of course not! They helped write all those laws; there's no way they could've broken them! They know the law back to front! Illegality? Pshaw!"

"What about making them sell some of those buildings to pay you back, or requiring them to pay a percentage of their profit to you?"

"Oh, I couldn't do that!" He looked shocked. "Why, they'd leave here in an instant and take all their money with them, and then where would I be? No, no, the only way is to help them out a little bit more and hope that will get things turned around properly. They keep telling me it'll all start trickling down eventually, and soon it'll be a gushing fountain of wealth! We just have to have faith."

"..."

"Why are you staring at me?"

"I just wanted to make sure I'd processed all of that correctly in my mind. No money; they'll take all their wealth; it's all completely legal—got it. Moving on!"

I tapped my fingers together under my chin, brow furrowed in concentration. "Now, this last question is important and should help me narrow down exactly who is the cause of your misfortune, so I need you to answer completely honestly."

He nodded eagerly, eyes alight with intensity at the thought of finally discovering the malefactor.

"How educated is your family?"

A quizzical expression flitted around his face before his features settled into a scowl. "Education? What the hell do you need to know that for? I don't see how that has anything to do with my problem; it's a case of theft, pure and simple!" He raised the revolver threateningly again, and I could see his finger tighten on the trigger.

"If you could humor me, please, I would greatly appreciate it. One must consider all the facts of a case before making a judgment."

A tense silence ensued for several seconds before he lowered the gun halfway; the scowl remained on his face. "Well, little Jack and Diane had five years of Sunday schooling and twelve years of high school, but they never really understood much more than their ABC's. They're good with the TV theme songs, though. My son Kennedy went to one of those fancy prep schools but got kicked out for molesting some poor girl—luckily, we found a good lawyer to hush that up. Think he graduated from Kennedy's school actually. Splendid fellow. The rest of the family doesn't really do a whole lot; they mainly study daytime talk shows. Did you know they do all kinds of science on those? DNA tests and everything."

"And yourself?"

He sighed heavily. "I graduated magna cum laude from MIT and Harvard, was captain of the debate team and president of the ethics club, and I'm a physician with fifteen different specialties. I also built a spaceship. The family—well, they don't seem to appreciate learning as much as I did. For the life of me, I can't figure out why." His expression grew morose.

"When the children were younger, I gave them all the stimulation they could ask for—television, movies, video games, the best nannies money could buy. I told them over and over how successful they would be if they could just master Wall Street or land in an advertising agency somewhere—look at all their cousins! But they just wanted to live off my achievements, skate by on my success—"

"And you let them?"

"They're family! If I don't take care of them all, some of them might not succeed, and then how would I be able to live with myself? I simply cannot believe how heartless you are! Should I let them fail when I have the means to provide for them? Clearly, you don't know the first thing about raising a dependent."

Sweat rivulets trickled down his brow as he finished yelling, and I leaned back in my chair, once again clasping my hands behind my head and stretching out my legs. The sun had slowly gone down during our conversation, and now the orange rays of dusk filled the office and dust motes danced in the air. I stared at him in silence for several minutes, watching him fidget and twitch. Finally, I spoke.

"After reviewing all the facts, both clear and unclear, it seems obvious to me who is responsible for your downward spiral, my good man. However, before we get to that conclusion, I have one more question for you."

I paused for a moment, taking in the haunting atmosphere of the fading light. There is a truly majestic quality in the shadows that overtake our world in such a regular rhythm, the ebb and flow as old as time. Who truly knows what lurks beneath darkness's mantle?

"Why are honest men so hard to find?" I asked.

He smiled, and tightened his finger on the trigger.

"Because," he said, "they keep telling me the truth."

It Ain't All Fame and Fortune

This piece originally ran on The Trenches *at http://trenchescomic
.com/tales/post/it-aint-all-fame-and-fortune.*

You want to hear some shit? Let me tell you about my average
day. It starts off with waking up at 6:45 in the morning, which is
waaaaaay before the sun comes up, which means it's cold. Real
cold. So cold that the steering-wheel heater in my BMW takes at
LEAST five minutes to warm up. Sometimes I even have to hit the
three-zone seat heater, which is not a step I take lightly. That thing
chews right through ultra-premium gas.

Once the climate problems are dealt with, I have to fight my
way through ten, maybe fifteen minutes of light traffic. Occasionally there's an accident, some person in an Oldsmobile or something, and I have to drop down to fifty-five miles an hour. Let me
tell you, there is nothing more depressing than driving past a

broken-down minivan filled with screaming children when you can only do fifty-five. Just awful.

Finally I get to work. My clothes are freshly laundered and hanging in my locker, but the industrial-strength drying machine they use shrinks my pants sometimes and then I have to ask for a new pair. They always give it to me, but it's just so humiliating to actually have to talk to the equipment managers. Rarely, they make eye contact, and what am I supposed to do then? Acknowledge them? Pretend to remember their names?

After the pants disaster, the only way to calm myself down is to head up to the cafeteria and order some freshly made pancakes and scrambled egg whites, but the kitchen staff create a very hostile environment. They also put out biscuits, gravy, waffles, hash browns, thick-cut bacon, thin-cut bacon, and sausage patties, and there's a fruit and yogurt bar, a cereal stand, croissants, English muffins, more bacon, and fully made breakfast sandwiches. How am I supposed to look at all that and eat healthy at the same time? Some people just don't get it.

Once breakfast is out of the way (and I've been forced to bus my own dishes over to the dishwasher), it's time for meetings. Then there's an agonizing forty-five minutes before I can finally escape, and if I fall asleep during the meetings, I get yelled at. It's so unfair—don't they know how early I have to wake up? Then I have to somehow find a way to fill the next two hours before lunch; usually the only option is to play dominoes, but sometimes I lose and that really sucks. It's super hard to stay focused at work once you lose a domino game. It can ruin your entire day.

After lunch (with a measly selection of four entrées, three side courses, a salad bar, a sandwich bar, a dessert bar, and an ice cream freezer), there's another hour of dead time that I'm supposed to fill.

Usually I'll sneak into the equipment room and read the paper, but the couch there is getting old, and the dryers are moderately loud, so it's a less-than-ideal environment. It's really hard to focus on the crossword puzzle with a dryer rattling around. Other times, I'll go take a nap in the lounge, but there's only the two couches, so if it fills up, it's a real bummer.

Then comes the worst part of the day: practice. I have to actually put on my cleats and go punt a football for THIRTY MINUTES.

Thirty minutes. I'll let that sink in a little bit.

Don't make the mistake of thinking that I'm done when the punting ends either—then I have to go inside and pretend to lift weights so I can sit down. The coaches don't let us sit down on the field, and I think you'll all agree that that's basically indentured servitude. I'm considering filing an OSHA complaint.

After all that grueling work, practice finally ends and I have to hurry up and head home at three so I can avoid traffic. Exhausting. My only relief is to sit on the couch and play games until midnight to unwind from the stress.

So when you video-game testers think you have it hard, in your air-conditioned rooms with your fancy electronics, take a minute and think about us poor NFL punters. We deal with the real shit, out in the real world. Our trenches run deep.

Just Deserts

You get the government you deserve.

What do I mean by this? Simple. The governing body of a country is a direct representation of what the citizenry of that country is willing to tolerate. Your government reflects you; it is the power-wielding mirror of your desires.

Right now in the United States, that mirror shines darkly. People may rail against the passage of bills like SOPA, PIPA, NDAA, and other rights-encroaching tyrannies of the state, but why are politicians proposing them in the first place?

The answer is: You let them. You decided that you'd rather have cheap mass-produced shit from Walmart or Target because it cost ten cents less to buy. You decided that the quick-cash grab of the housing bubble was worth fucking the economy; that trucks that get eight miles to the gallon were a good idea and to hell with the environment; that being in a union automatically entitled you to cushy benefits and the right to just show up and put in your time because who gives a fuck if that road gets finished three days from now or three weeks from now, you're getting paid either way, and—oh, whoops, another bridge fell down.

You decided that your instant gratification was worth ignoring the long-term problems that corporate-manufacturing abuse of the environment entails. You decided that global warming was just some nonsense cooked up by crackpot tree-humpers, never mind that 99 fucking percent of the scientific community agrees that it's a serious problem with serious consequences that we need to address NOW. You decided you'd rather pay $500 million for another hundred cruise missiles than fund scientific exploration and education and teach your children about the future.

You know what else you decided? You decided that money was more important than intelligence. You decided that being smart was something to be afraid of rather than something to be celebrated. You decided your role models were athletes and reality-TV stars, not scientists and philosophers. I mean, who gives a shit about Socrates when you can watch the Situation, amirite?

And you know what? You can't deny this, because that's the government we have. We have politicians whose only concern is money and how they can use it to get reelected and what kind of pork they can funnel over to their states. We have Supreme Court justices who think that a faceless conglomeration of ideas that exists solely to make money should have the same rights as a person but without any of the responsibilities like, oh, taxes and accountability. We have presidents who start wars without considering the ramifications of what will happen based on information they didn't want to have to think too hard about. We have bills and laws and detention centers where we've shat upon the things this country was founded on, things like the right to a speedy trial and the right not to be tortured. We have literal war criminals (as defined by the Geneva convention, which we are very much a signatory to) living in this country who no one has the goddamned balls to prosecute, because God forbid someone gets his feelings hurt that the people he supported turned out to be power-grubbing assholes. We have the audacity of hope and the reality of business as usual, thanks so much for the vote, hope you enjoy your vacation in Guantanamo.

So complain all you want, but until you decide to educate yourself, until you develop the will to learn, until you see other people as human beings and not as objects to be exploited, until you realize that settling for the banal mediocrity of mindless consumption is the root cause of all your problems—well, until that day, you'll keep getting the government you deserve.

Just Call Me Thomas

Atheists confuse me. It takes just as much faith to claim something unknowable isn't real as it does to proclaim it's real. The only way you'd know for certain, one way or the other, would be to step outside the universe so you could see how everything ticks along and how it all fits together, and at that point, you've effectively become God. It's a little like opening the box with the crowbar packed inside it.

Me? I'm cheerfully agnostic. I like to look at the universe and learn new things, and the only way I can do that is by keeping open the possibility that I just may be terribly wrong about everything I thought was right. I have faith in the ability of the universe to constantly surprise me, to throw my mental gears for such a loop that the only response is to laugh at the wonderful absurdity of it all. Just the other day, I learned that a person's colon can explode during a colonoscopy. How is that even a thing?! What will I learn tomorrow?

My religion is doubt. I believe with all my heart that I will never know everything, that the decisions I make will necessarily be flawed by the imperfect assumptions I base them on but that the only way to keep learning is to change those assumptions when faced with new evidence.

Exploding colonoscopies. Isn't that just something.

I'm not a big believer in fate. To me, fate is a copout. It's a way to absolve yourself of responsibility for your own actions; in essence, to deny your own humanity by turning yourself into an automaton, a mindless slave.

Fuck fate. Fuck fate and its cold-iron shackles wearing our legs raw as we trudge in the same blind circle. Fuck fate and the numb cattle-like torpor it causes. Fuck fate and every single tyrant who's ever tried to enslave someone.

I choose free will. I choose to believe that my actions have meaning, my thoughts validity, and my dreams reality. I choose my right to make this world a better place for all those who would rise up against fate's blind yoke and CHOOSE to take responsibility for their actions, knowing full well it means they must examine the consequences of those actions.

Why? Because if I'm fated to act like this, at least it lets me spit in the old bastard's eye.

A Brief Interlude

The temperature at kickoff is predicted to be a balmy 72 degrees with a light breeze from the southeast. Playing in today's Equality Bowl are the Lustful Cockmonsters, winners of this year's Fromunda League, and the Beautifully Unique Sparkleponies, champions of the Sad Trombone Division. I'll tell you what—you've never seen such resplendent uniforms as the ones these two teams are wearing. It's almost like watching a clown filled with confetti explode in slow motion while Richard Simmons backflips his way through a triple rainbow.

Early picks have the Lustful Cockmonsters as five-point favorites, the team resurgent behind the potent combination of Hamshank Thunderloin and Drake Crotchcrusher, but some experts predict that the high-flying aerial attack of Lily "Donkeypunch" Landon and Jupiter Cameltoe could lead the Sparkleponies to an upset. Of course, the player fans are most eager to see, Fister

McGrundle, appears to have suffered some sort of lower-leg injury following an unusually energetic bout of calisthenics during pre-game warm-up. We'll update you as we learn more; I know I speak for everyone at the stadium when I say that a game without a good Fister is simply not worth watching.

Also in the mix are field conditions. While initial reports were favorable about the beautifully manicured and styled grass, a brief shower of glitter and tinsel appears to have made the footing a bit treacherous. As we speak, equipment managers are breaking out the stiletto heels and workmen's boots to give the players a little extra traction if they need it.

Stay tuned for moooooooooore SPORTSBALL!

How to Win the Internet in Seven Easy Steps

Step 1. Connect to the Internet. If you're logging on through AOL's thirty-day free trial CD, please, for the love of all that's holy, do not try to Win the Internet. I promise you that it won't end well.

Step 2. Find something that makes you upset. This can be literally anything at all. Did *Cat Fancy* publish a scathing review of "long-haired Siamese whatever the hell *Cat Fancy* calls a cat"? Begin wildly gesticulating as you spit frothing obscenities at your monitor. Is someone in an obscure chili subforum at BobsChili Hut.com extolling the virtues of beanless chili? Let your blood pressure hit 500 psi while your pacemaker issues sad beeping noises. Did your local sportsball player fail your impossible goals of perfection by showing himself to be only mortal? Better get a mouth guard so you don't shatter your teeth into a fine powder as you grind them together in rage.

Step 3. Write down why you're upset. Since the medium of print doesn't convey volume or emotion very well, you'll have to make up for it by using CAPS LOCK AND MISSPELLING/ TRUNCATING AS MNY WOORDS ASD POSIBLE!!!1! The key is to ride that fine edge of literacy and lunacy; you want the lucky recipient of your righteous judgment to feel the weight of every thundering denunciation, but if it's too incomprehensible, the guy'll probably just ignore it.

Step 4. Post the ten-page essay you just wrote about your chosen victim's mating habits (generally with corpses or wild animals), personal hygiene (nonexistent), family lineage (whores and baby molesters), intelligence (dumber than a lobotomized clam on bath salts), and genitalia (scabrous, pustulant, and disfigured) anywhere you think he could possibly see it. This includes Facebook, Twitter, Reddit, personal blogs, impersonal blogs, random news aggregators, and printed broadsides.

Step 5. Wait for your target to respond. When he does, take select quotations completely out of context to back up whatever point you feel like making while maintaining a continuous barrage of ad hominem attacks. If he raises a valid point you don't want to address, either pretend it was never said or claim that he misinterpreted you and obviously isn't smart enough to understand your logic. Continue berating the individual until he refuses to answer anymore or until the quoting and requoting causes the page to crash and drag down half of Geocities with it. Bonus points for saying, "Clearly I can't have a conversation with someone as intolerant as you—I'm through here" and then continuing the argument.

Step 6. Eat a victory snack, secure in the knowledge that you definitely changed the mind of someone you'll never meet in real life. There's no doubt he's a million times more fulfilled now that you've educated him on his various inadequacies and shared how they can be corrected. If only everyone in the world were as smart as you, we'd all Win the Internet!

Step 7. Self-euthanize.

Introspection

This is the part where I tell you about me.

Growing up, I was always the nerdy kid with thick glasses who knew all the answers and eagerly waved his hand in class. It wasn't to make others feel bad or to try to get attention; as children, we're taught that it's a good thing to learn and have the right answers. I enjoy excelling at things, and I had the answers (most of the time, though I thought I had them all the time), so I raised my hand. I still raise my hand if there's a question I can answer. I guess I like sharing information with people.

Growing up, I was the best player on my soccer and baseball teams; I pitched and batted cleanup in baseball, and I played midfield and goalie in soccer. Part of my aptitude was due to the various baseball and soccer camps my parents sent me to, and the other part was that I enjoyed excelling at things. I liked to compete and I liked to win, and I still do; I will never apologize for that. I'm fundamentally incapable of giving anything less than my best effort, so bear that in mind if you invite me to a Ping-Pong match or a game of Warmachine (I've learned how to be less of a jerk about it, though, which I'm pretty sure is a good thing).

Growing up, I always had my head in a book. I mastered the art of reading while walking: I glanced up quickly every now and then to make sure I didn't run into anything. I loved to read, and I would frequently get in trouble in class for reading when I was supposed to be paying attention. This seemed rather odd to me at the time (and still does), but whatever. Apparently, school is for learning what the curriculum says you should learn, not for learning in and of itself. I would also read in the car on the way to soccer and baseball practice, in the bathtub, under my covers late at night when I was supposed to be sleeping (I had to develop a good ear to hear my mom coming up the stairs to catch me); basically, whenever I had some free time, I was reading. People who know me now will say nothing has changed in that respect.

Growing up, I had no idea what girls were for. I could talk with them, build sand castles with them, and play board games with them, but the concept of relationships never even entered my mind. I didn't go on a date until my senior year of high school, and that was more because it seemed to be the expected thing to do (I was slowly picking up civilized manners at that point, but the going was rough). I went on recruiting trips to UCLA, and when I was there, I was completely clueless that my future wife was at all interested in me; I just thought she was being nice by explaining the different things to do once I got to campus. (We're both pretty glad that I figured it out eventually.) I asked to go to an arcade during my official visit because the basketball game was boring and I wanted to do something fun. Nothing out of the ordinary about that, right?

Growing up, I got in fights with my brother all the time. We were both completely unwilling to back down from anything, and that led to some truly interesting incidents (I maintain that I never started a single one; I just finished it). We can look at those now and chuckle, but we've both had to learn how to walk away, a lesson I think is valuable no matter what age you learn it. You should never be afraid to stand your ground for something worth fighting for, but learning what's worth fighting for can be a very long (and occasionally painful) process. Nowadays I let the little stuff go; life's too short to be angry all the time, and I'd rather laugh at the absurdity of it all. Fair warning, though—don't mess with my sense of justice; there's some vicious monsters lurking in those depths, and when they come out, well, there be dragons.

Growing up, I had parents who loved me (and they still do). They taught me to be polite, to always give my best effort, and to treat other people the way I would want to be treated. They gave me the tools I needed to succeed in life even if I didn't realize it at the time, and, really, what child does? I hated practicing the violin, but now I know that I have an ear for music because of that practice. I hated practicing soccer and baseball, but now I know that the only way to succeed is to put in the necessary hard work. I hated not being able to play video games all the time, but now I know that everything in moderation is the key to a happy, healthy life. I've made my own choices in that life, but the scaffolding and structure of those choices was made available to me by my parents, and for that I love them.

Growing up, I had a family that cared, and that's all a child needs.

A List

This is a brief list of things that annoy me. Scratch that—not annoy me; *infuriate* me. Teeth-clenching, sweat-inducing rage triggers. If you're on this list, I HATE YOU and I hope you sit on a tack.

People Who Lean Their Seats Back on Airplanes

Hey, pickletits, you know what? I'm six feet five inches tall, and I ALREADY DON'T FIT IN THIS FLYING SARDINE TIN. When you oh-so-merrily tilt back to get an extra couple of inches of leg-room for your five-foot-eight-inch frame, I want to strangle you with the strap of your Coach bag. I was already flossing with my kneecaps before you started invading my space, and it's literally all I can do not to rip off the tray table and beat you savagely about the head and shoulders until you return to the upright position. I know the seat's uncomfortable, but you leaning it back won't suddenly turn it into a recliner, and your blithe ignorance of human anatomy (as regards the length of tibiae and the bending of knee joints) makes Bad Thoughts percolate through my brain. Also, it crunches down my laptop screen, so I get the added bonus of dislocating my spine if I try to watch anything on it.

Don't be a dick. Leave your seat alone and suffer through the flight like the rest of us, because I can guarantee you I'm going to kick the back of it like a hyperactive five-year-old until you figure things out (*kick* being a relative term, given my complete inability to move anything below the shoulders, so I'll have to settle for a pointed knee jab as I fruitlessly try to find a more comfortable position).

People Who Zoom Ahead on the Shoulder of the Road When There's Traffic So They Can Cut in Front of Everyone Else When It's Time to Merge

You guys are assholes, plain and simple. Do you really think the rest of us are sitting bumper to bumper listening to shitty music while the sun broils us alive inside our cars because we enjoy it? No, we don't enjoy it. In fact, it really sucks. We're sitting here slowly contemplating a re-creation of *Falling Down* but not driving on the side of the road, because we learned this amazing concept in kindergarten called WAIT YOUR FUCKING TURN, YOU TROGLODYTE. We know there's a merge up ahead. We saw the signs! Apparently, though, it's too much to ask for any of you guys to follow the same goddamn rules of the road as everyone else, so we get to wait an extra twenty minutes while you scream past in your custom flame-decal F-350 with a three-foot lift as Nickelback blares forth like an apocalyptic clarion call and then nudge your way in front of some terrified housewife who's a shattered wreck for the next three days.

Every single time I see one of you syphilitic toads, I take great pleasure in pulling in front of you and then proceeding to travel at exactly two miles an hour. Keep laying on the horn—I might just let other people pass me so you get back from your power lunch even later! You're a festering jizzstain and I hope your urethra gets invaded by poisonous spiders. Oh, and those truck nutz? Not as hilarious as you think they are.

People Who Play Music Really Loud on Their Phones without Benefit of Headphones in the Mistaken Assumption Everyone Else Wants to Listen to Autotuned Ear Poison

Look, I get it. You're a fan of some obscure indie-folk-funk-trailer rock-narwhal yodeler who records only through a Fisher-Price cat keyboard while applying fifteen different effects pedals at once. That's great. I'm happy for you. Now I'd like to introduce you to this amazing new invention called PUT SOME HEADPHONES ON BEFORE I MURDER YOUR FACE WITH A HAM.

I don't want to hear your crappy music! If I wanted to hear your crappy music, I'd go buy it and listen to it, and the fact that I haven't should give you a very solid clue that I'm not interested in the soothing strains of Bespoke Dildonics. Do you really think your mad iTunes DJ skills are going to make a party suddenly appear (possibly with Bud Light and a bewildered Pitbull)? No! Stop polluting the air in a forty-five-meter radius because you just have to share the latest underground club hit from Lil' Big Yolo, because if you don't, I'm going to pull up some crap by Smashing

Pumpkins that sounds like a violin being run through Satan's asshole and make us all miserable.

(Also, if your headphones are Beats by Dre, that shit doesn't count. Those are useless for actually keeping noise contained in the ear canal. Seriously, there're old-school boom boxes that are quieter.)

People Who Touch You Uncomfortably During Conversations

Aghgh! Stop it! No one enjoys it when you stroke someone's forearm while expounding earnestly on the merits of double flushing, or when you drape your arm over a guy's shoulder while going over the TPS report. It's gross, it's creepy, and it's really not cool, man. Notice how I'm not humping your leg while we're having a conversation? Extend the same respect to me, please. If I wanted to be touched inappropriately, I'd go drop some soap in the prison shower, but we're fully dressed in the middle of an Applebee's, so knock it off.

People with Vanity License Plates *and* Handicapped Stickers on Their Corvettes

Seriously. We all know you got that handicapped placard from your doctor buddy whom you have a five-martini lunch with every Thursday out at the golf course, and when I have to walk by BGMONEY or PWRPLYR parked in the disabled spot, I want to take a nine iron to your scrotum, especially when you come running out of Starbucks because you're late for your tee time. You're a giant fraud, and if there's any justice in the universe, one day your car will run over your ankles so you'll actually qualify for that sticker. I hope your triple latte sets your upholstery on fire, and your wife runs off with the cabana boy.

People Who Constantly Try to One-Up You in Their Stories

"Oh, that's amazing, you came in second place in your track meet, just super; did I ever tell you about the time I won the Boston Marathon while running backward and suffering from Ebola? It wasn't really a big deal, I only spent two years training under the Dalai Lama to focus my seventeen core chakras, reaching a level he said he'd never seen before, but I have to say, I think it definitely helped me nail that Oscar-winning role in the remake of *Les Mis* I starred in—no, not the one they premiered at the Guggenheim, that place is sooooo overrated, ours was at this eco-friendly fair-trade village that was built for starving African orphans with typhus, and it was absolutely marvelous—life-altering, even. Why are you grabbing that baseball bat?"

People Who Make Lists

Just absolute wastes of oxygen. Think they're so special with their itemized descriptions and clever bullet-point formatting. Douches.

XY

One chromosome. That's all it takes to change how the world perceives you as a human being. Somehow, this one chromosome determines how much money you'll make, how much freedom you'll be allowed to have, how much education or knowledge people think your brain can hold.

Why?

Why do we place so much emphasis on one chromosome? Why have we, for so long, decided that this one chromosome is the only way to judge a person's worth? What is it about having a dick that makes so many people act like one?

I'll tell you why. It's because we value strength over empathy. We think that the ability to apply physical force is the defining measure of humanity, when in fact it's our ability to work together and protect the value of the mind no matter the body it resides in that has made us the dominant species on the planet.

Any jackass can apply the threat of violent coercion. It doesn't take intelligence to menace someone with a club, to point a gun and demand submission. It takes intelligence to realize why doing so is ultimately harmful to the fabric of society, that without the protection of freedom and life, we will all drag ourselves back down to rocks and sticks.

Don't buy into the hype. Don't think that because you happened to be born a man, you somehow have the right to tell other people what to do. Don't think that a single chromosome gives you the right to invalidate someone else's free will, to take away anyone's choices and opportunities.

XX, XY, XYZ, and beyond—none of it makes a single bit of difference when compared to how someone acts, how someone behaves, how someone reveals his or her true identity time and time again. Man, woman, or whatever the future may hold— nothing gives you the right to enslave someone else.

One chromosome. What is that, when weighed against your very humanity?

Motes and Beams

Dear Archbishop Nienstedt and Pope Benedict XVI,[1]

"Blessed are they who are persecuted for righteousness' sake; for theirs is the kingdom of heaven."

"But if ye forgive not men their trespasses, neither will your Father forgive your trespasses."

"Judge not, that ye be not judged. For with what judgment ye judge, ye shall be judged; and with what measure ye mete, it shall be measured to you again."

I read your views on gay marriage in the *Star Tribune*, Archbishop Nienstedt, and it fills me with great sadness and regret that a steward of the Catholic Church on this Earth feels the need to take a stance of oppression, intolerance, and fear.

Surely, is this not what Jesus spoke of when he said, "Either make the tree good and his fruit good; or else make the tree corrupt, and his fruit corrupt; for the tree is known by his fruit"?

How can we reconcile our vision of the Catholic Church as salvation to the sick, the needy, and the poor with this demonstration of the Catholic Church as oppressor, tormentor, and executioner? Where in all of Jesus's teachings did he ever say to deny the humanity of other human beings? Where did the Son of God proclaim that mortal man knew God's will? Where, pray tell, did Jesus ever say one should harden his heart against those who may not be exactly the same as him?

I say to you—nowhere. Nowhere does Jesus preach hate, or intolerance, or loathing. Nowhere does Jesus say, "You shall deny the humanity of gay people because they make you feel uncomfortable." Nowhere does Jesus say, "And the mortal men of the Church shall be the sole conduits of the Word of God, for they are perfect and infallible." Nowhere in all of the recorded teachings of Jesus does it say anything about discrimination or prejudice.

"But whoso shall offend one of these little ones which believe in me, it were better for him that a millstone were hanged about his neck, and that he were drowned in the depth of the sea."

Millions of children are being raised in the Catholic faith. Some of these children will be gay, not through any choice of their own, but because that is how God created them. What does it say to those children when the head of their religion in this diocese, a man who claims to "explain and defend the teaching of the Church because I have been ordained to do so and I believe those teachings with all my heart," a man acting under the auspices of the pope himself, tells them that they are less worthy than some others, even though they believe in the teachings of Jesus? What will these children think as they suffer the barbed insults of their classmates and teachers? I ask you, sir, what will these children think as they are belittled and tormented due to teachings you espouse? What judgment will be passed on *your* soul when yet another poor child reaches for the knife or the noose to end the earthly torment he or she has been subjected to because of your example?

Do you presume to speak for God, Archbishop Nienstedt? Will you tell these children, faithful children who attend Sunday school and earnestly pray every day, that they are somehow less than others in God's eyes? Will you grasp that millstone, Archbishop Nienstedt, clasp it all the way to the bottom, clutching at the heavy weight of earthly power and influence, even as it drags you down?

"No man can serve two masters: for either he will hate the one, and love the other; or else he will hold to the one, and despise the other. Ye cannot serve God and mammon."

"Then saith he unto them, Render therefore unto Caesar the things which are Caesar's; and unto God the things that are God's."

Tell me, Archbishop, Pope, what purpose does it serve for the Church to attempt to influence the affairs of a secular state? The federal benefits under law that are currently denied gay couples certainly fall under the realm of things that are Caesar's, don't they? No one is forcing the Catholic Church to marry gay couples if that is not the Church's wish. You can keep the sanctity of Catholic marriage solely between heterosexual couples if you feel that is what's required (again, though, I caution you on the dangers of presumed infallibility). All I am asking is for you to extend the open hand of tolerance, not the closed fist of fear and hate. As American citizens, we respect everyone's right to practice whatever religion (if any) he or she chooses to. Haven't we learned enough from the Crusades, the Inquisitions, the Talibans of the world? What does it benefit the Church to attempt to influence secular policy in this country, especially when that policy is a denial of some people's basic human rights? Will you now assume Caesar's throne, grasping the ephemera of worldly power and control while forsaking the eternal kingdom of Heaven?

All I ask of you, Archbishop Nienstedt, and of you, Pope Benedict XVI, is that you practice that most basic teaching found in the Bible—empathy. If you strike me, I shall turn the other cheek. If you ask me to walk with you for a mile, I will go with you two. If you ask me to respect your faith, your beliefs, then all I ask is that you do the same for everyone else. For is that not the most pertinent of Jesus's teachings, and one that everyone, no matter his religion, can strive to achieve?

"Jesus said unto him, Thou shalt love the Lord thy God with all thy heart, and with all thy soul, and with all thy mind. This is the first and great commandment. *And the second is like unto it, Thou shalt love thy neighbor as thyself.*

"On these two commandments hang all the law and the prophets."

---

[1] Note: this piece written prior to Pope Benedict XVI resigning his position on February 28, 2013.

Some Other People Have Even More Trouble with Logic

This piece was originally written in response to an opinion letter penned to the Minneapolis Star Tribune by one Mr. Riley Balling, an attorney (I'm assuming he has paperwork to back up that claim somewhere).

Balling's point can be summed up in the following paragraph from his editorial: "For many of us who favor traditional marriage, marriage is about raising children in a healthy environment. Thus, any change to the definition of marriage affects our marriage. Our 'traditional' marriages and the children they produce are our greatest source of happiness, and we desire that our children will live in a world that will promote their ability to make the same choices that brought us happiness."

You can find his piece here *(curse you hypertext links not working in physical media formats!): http://www.startribune.com/opinion/commentaries/171613511.html. If you don't want to bother looking it up (and I don't blame you if you don't), he basically said, "WARGLEBLARGLE GAY PEOPLES ARE RUININ' MY MARRIAGES" and then forgot to provide examples.*

Dear Mr. Balling,

I read your opinion piece in today's *Star Tribune,* and I would like to take a brief moment to offer you some assistance in your future writing endeavors. I can only assume that you've never been trained in classical logic, debate techniques, or basic empathy, so I will humbly offer my own meager knowledge in these fields as it relates to your literary masterpiece "Why Same-Sex Marriage Affects My Marriage."

You start off strong, with an opening salvo ostensibly proclaiming that every group has the right to its own views (if we ignore the fearmongering subhead of the article, "The goal is to move society—in this case, away from a safe environment for children"), but then, much like a Michael Bay plot, your argument starts careening off the rails. Your first mistake is what is termed a mind-projection fallacy—the assumption that the way you see the world is the way the world really is.

You state, "As we have seen, and understandably so, people in homosexual relationships are trying to change society to more readily embrace and promote their view of their identity. This is possible largely due to the disassociation between sexual relationships and procreation." But what you're really saying is "Those gay people do sex things that I find icky, and we should oppress them because they can't have babies." You completely ignore the fact that homosexual people are trying to change society not just because they want to have teh butt secks (or rise and grind, for the ladies), but also because they want to avoid, oh, I don't know, things like homosexuals being tortured and tied to a fence post until they die (Matthew Shepard), shot to death while attending school (Lawrence King), shot to death for being transgender (Moses King), committing suicide by hanging due to repeated bullying and taunting (Carl Joseph Walker-Hoover), shot to death and burned while standing military guard (Seaman August Provost), and stabbed to death after serving in the Vietnam War (James Zappalorti). Every single one of these attacks occurred because of the victim's sexuality. Let's not even get into the over eleven hundred federal benefits gay couples are legally unable to obtain in the state of Minnesota because they can't get married—things like health care, survivor benefits, and legacies to pass on to their families (including children).

Deep breath.

Moving on, we come to the next little pearl of wisdom hidden in your manifesto, that hoary old chestnut of traditional marriage. In this case, you've made the logic error of the etymological fallacy: the assumption that the original or historical meaning of a word or phrase is necessarily similar to its current meaning.

Which version of the term *traditional marriage* would you like to use, Mr. Balling? Should we go back to ancient Israel and practice polygamy, in which the only right a woman had was the right to own her own tent? Or should we use the ancient Greek definition of *marriage*, one more concerned with inheritance than with love, one that forced a woman to divorce her current husband and marry a sibling if that was required to continue the family? Should we force a brother to marry his dead sibling's wife? Or perhaps we should make arranged marriages with child brides; that's certainly traditional enough. Wait, I know, let's go with the one where you have to pay three goats and a cow in order to ensure the woman is yours to keep forever, and you can stone her to death if she cheats on you. That one sounds terrific!

You see, Mr. Balling, since you don't actually provide a definition of the term *traditional marriage*, I think your definition of it boils down to "I want to make people who believe differently than I do miserable by taking away their free will, so I'll cloak my hate in the guise of *tradition* and *history* without knowing what those words really mean," and, well, I'm not really okay with that. Also, traditional marriage has traditionally been rather tough on 50 percent of the human population, what with the whole enslavement and forced-childbearing and stoning-to-death thing (I'm talking about women, if you haven't figured it out [sorry to the people who figured it out like five minutes ago, but I wanted to make sure he got it]), and I'm not really okay with that either.

Deep breath. <whelps!>

Your third logic fallacy—and, oh boy, does this one crop up a lot—is that of *cum hoc, ergo propter hoc.* Now, I'm guessing your Latin may be a little rusty (although it may not be, in which case, well done!), so if you need help, I'd like to ask the entire class to say it along with me: CORRELATION DOES NOT IMPLY CAUSATION.

You can't make the statement "Bless the single parents who try, but there is a direct correlation between single homes and crimes of all types" and not expect every moderately intelligent person to jump all over it. Single-parent homes don't *cause* crime. That's like saying, "I rode my bicycle to work today, and it rained, therefore my bicycle causes rain." There are a multitude of factors related to crime, including income, residence location, public resources available, education, education available, age demographics, police presence, temperature patterns, et cetera, ad nauseam, ad infinitum (which means I could go on for a while [also, way to take a giant steaming literary dump on every single parent, infertile couple, and those people who choose not to have kids; you're making all sorts of friends today]). To single out single parents is, to put it bluntly, absolutely absurd.

And then, to make it even better, you manage to link an unsafe environment for children (somehow caused by single parents?) to same-sex marriage by claiming same-sex marriage "reinforces changes to the marital definition." Hoo-boy. Tell me: Were you worried about the children when all those colored folks started marrying the white people? Because that sure was a change to the "marital definition," and, funnily enough, there were a bunch of people using this same argument back then. Or how about when women started working? Are the kids unsafe now because Mom wanted to actually do something with her life instead of putting on a plastic smile and tending to the kitchen all day? (No offense to any stay-at-home moms or dads who choose to do so; I know that's a full-time job in itself, and you have my respect.) What happened when the "marital definition" changed to allow divorce and remarrying? Should we pass some constitutional amendments preventing those? C'mon, don't stop with the gays; go oppress a bunch of other people too!

AND THEN, to make it even more betterer (grammars!), you return to the mind-projection fallacy by claiming, "Currently, as a society, we have wavered from this traditional motivation, and many, not all, view marriage as a venue for self-fulfillment." It's so nice of you, Mr. Balling, to define my and countless others' marriages as a "venue for self-fulfillment." Oddly, though, I don't remember you ever hanging out with my family and me, or with our neighbors, so I don't see how you could provide any sort of factual information to back up your claim. (And if you say that I need to provide evidence so you can disprove it, that's called *onus probandi*, in case you were interested.) The only fact that I've been able to glean from your entire ill-constructed argument is that you don't know how to construct an argument. You know, with facts and stuff. (The basis of your argument is what's called an appeal to emotion— more specifically, it's an appeal to fear—if you wanted that for future reference.)

Deep breath. <1 percent, don't wipe now!>

Frankly, sir, your blatant attempt to sway people by using the "OH MAH GAWD, THINK OF THE CHILDREN" argument is tiresome, bothersome, and insulting, and anyone who has the slightest interest in doing so can pull aside your curtain of self-satisfied drivel and expose the ugliness underneath. Furthermore, you never made any sort of logical attempt to explain how same-sex marriage affects your marriage in any concrete way, instead offering up vague generalizations with no proof. When it comes to the children, I can assure you that I *am* thinking of my children, and not just my children but all the children they will come in contact with and all the adults they will someday be, and it is my sincerest wish as a parent that I can raise them to be tolerant, to respect the free will of others, and, above all, to be able to see beneath the smug bigotry and oppression of those who would enslave the world to satisfy their own ugly lust for control. If you have any children, it is my hope that they enjoy a peaceful life, one free of tyranny.

Aaaaaaaaand *fin.*

Somebody Think of the Children

I would like to share some of the things I thought were important from the Vote No gathering I recently attended.

1. Gay people are exactly the same as straight people. They laughed, they yelled, they congratulated me on the Vikings winning, they told me they rooted for the Saints, they spilled beer on the floor and apologized for doing so. They asked for autographs, shook my hand, posed for pictures, and introduced me to their significant others. They talked about how excited they were for the Vikings' season this year, told me how long they've been season-ticket holders, and asked if I thought that Ponder kid was going to be any good (I said yes). At no point was I excessively fondled and at no time did a bacchanalian riot threaten the chastity of

my pants fasteners. In short, it was American citizens doing American activities in a quintessentially American way.

2. Gay people are not treated as American citizens. The number of individuals who came up and thanked Brendon and me for taking a stand was staggering and, frankly, depressing. I use the word *depressing* because if so many have to thank us for showing basic empathy, thank us for recognizing that they are human beings just like everyone else, that means that many, many other people have not. What that says about our society makes me ill, and it means that we are failing the American dream. America is supposed to be where people go to escape oppression, to escape persecution, to escape tyranny; sure, we haven't always gotten it right over the years, but we should always strive for that elusive goal of equality. Right now, we're just not getting it done.

3. One conversation that I had will stick with me for the rest of my life. It involved a local high school teacher and coach. He walked up, introduced himself, shook my hand, and said these exact words: "I want to thank you for speaking up. What you did will save children's lives."

This really hit me, in a primal way I was not expecting. A man who interacts with our youth every day, who sees their struggles and their triumphs and their failures, told me that my words meant a child might find hope instead of despair, might dare to believe he could be accepted for who he is.

Do you know how exceedingly ANGRY PUMA GROWL that is? A child should *never* have to feel that way. A child should *never* think that suicide is the only option, the only solution to the tormenting and bullying and unthinking viciousness adults often unwittingly pass along to the young. A child should *never* become a casualty in a war of oppression, of bigotry, of petty small-mindedness.

Because, make no mistake, children who suffer this way are casualties. All the hopes, all the dreams, all the wonderful potential life has in store are as dust before the scouring winds of intolerance (whether it be racist, sexist, or religious). Every time you propagate the message that a person who is gay is less than human, that same-sex marriage cannot be as filled with love and laughter and tears as heterosexual marriage, that gays don't deserve to pass a legacy on to their families, you quicken that howling storm and sweep away a tiny bit more humanity from the world, drive one more child to contemplating the cold razor's bite or the yawning abyss of the overdose because he or she simply cannot deal with the unceasing assault upon the psyche.

Well, I, for one, will not stand for it. I will not stand for a world that demeans those it finds "different" or "gross." I will not stand for an ideology that promotes slavish adherence to a single arbitrary standard, that sacrifices children on the altar of oppression and control. I will not stand for one more RED-TINGED-MUSHROOM-CLOUD second of people thinking that they have the right to live other people's lives for them, of the complete lack of empathy so often shown in our society.

I stand for gay marriage. I stand for the end of segregation. I stand for a woman's right to choose, both whom she votes for and what is done to her body. I stand for equality under the law, for treating others how I would want to be treated, for the fundamental human right to live a happy life free of tyranny.

I stand for my children.

Clearly I've matured greatly as I've aged.

This shirt is a great indication of my future job.

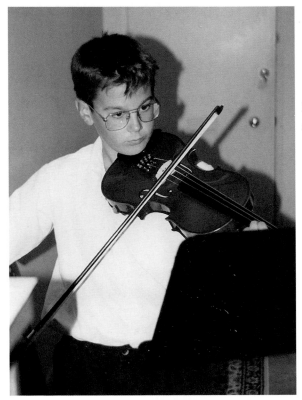

Rock star? Rock star.

[*Raspy cancer voice*] I am the SantaBatman.

Basically the coolest person ever.

I'll read anywhere. Couch, car, untamed wilds—whatever.

My dislike of shoes
started early.

The natural.

I don't whut even.

Best parent ever.

This is my sister. She's obviously impressed by my fashion sense.

Building a Super Star Destroyer is sweaty work. Manly work.

I, for one, welcome our new ant overlords, and our offspring who ride them.

Much to the chagrin of many same-sex marriage opponents, I do, in fact, have a family.

For teh Lulz

The year is 2065, and the world hovers in an uneasy peace; 3D printers, capable of creating almost anything the mind can imagine, are used to manufacture everything, including weapons. All anyone needs to do to obtain a gun is download the appropriate program from the Internet. Despite this, no gun has been fired in anger in ten years, owing to a vast surveillance program called the Panopticon that senses any imminent violence and activates a weapon's safety mechanism, disabling it thoroughly and immediately. There're still a lot of weapons, though.

Two men exchange furtive looks across a narrow strip of no-man's-land. Each man lies artfully concealed in a shallow fortification, his gun pointed unhesitatingly toward the other. They're both armed with AK-69s, which is the only assault rifle printed anymore, due to its cheap material cost and overall reliability. Both are on a hair trigger — earlier this morning, they separately received news from their respective high commands that the Panopticon would be going down at three o'clock that afternoon, and hostilities might possibly commence. There wasn't really a solid reason given for why hostilities might commence, but judging by the high command's tone of voice and word selection, each man sees clearly that commencing is the desired outcome.

Sweat trickles down the chin of the man in the northern bunker. His timepiece reads one minute until three. He shifts slightly and zeros his sights in on the bridge of the other man's nose. He can see his adversary doing the same to him.

Thirty seconds.

Fifteen seconds.

Five. Four. Three. Two. One. Suddenly, the first man's earpiece squawks and a voice cries out, "It's down! It's down! Take the shot! Quick, do it now!" The line goes dead.

He wastes no time and tightens his finger around the trigger, preparing to fire the first live round directed at another person in ten years. The occasion will no doubt be regarded as historic in some future history book. In the split second before the trigger depresses all the way, he can see his opponent's finger tightening as well, eyes narrowed in concentration.

Click.

Nothing happens. No bullet goes racing out, no metal slug comes tearing into his head. Confused, he pulls the trigger several more times. *Click. Click. Click.* The gun still won't fire. He hits it several times with his fist, but nothing—it's dead as a doornail.

He turns his attention back to the man lying in the other bunker and notices he's trying to get his weapon to work also. Gradually, the other man gives it up and looks across the short distance separating the two. Their eyes lock, and then they both shrug sheepishly and stand up, throwing aside the camouflage blankets that cover their revetments. They slowly amble toward each other and meet in the middle of the clearing.

"So..."

"Yours not working either?"

"Nope, darn thing won't fire. Ammo's loaded properly, I made sure the safety was off, but nothing."

"Same over here. I think I'm going to run another one off the printer, make sure it didn't skip any lines of code or anything."

"Yeah, that sounds like a good plan. I'll go try mine."

The two men separate and walk back to their bunkers. Each one puts in an order for a new AK-69, and they find themselves drifting back to the clearing while the guns are printing.

"So, uh, got any kids?"

"Yeah, a boy and a girl, twins. They'll be turning nine next month. How about you?"

"Only one, a girl; she's seven. Cutest little thing, nose like a button. Here's a picture."

"Very cute. I see what you mean. She looks like she has your eyes."

"Yeah, but luckily she got my wife's face."

They chuckle as two distant *dings* announce the printers have come to a halt. Both men turn and head back once again. Upon arrival, each man pulls out a brand-new AK-69, loads in a full clip of freshly printed bullets, and then settles down to draw a bead on the other. Out of courtesy, each one makes sure the other is set properly, and then their fingers close on their triggers at the same time.

Click-click.

The soft sound of metal sliding home is the only noise ringing across the battlefield. Both men stand up and, by unspoken consent, walk out to the middle once more, their guns casually leaning on their shoulders.

"Well, now, this is just weird."

"Tell me about it. These are supposed to be the most reliable guns in existence. I know it printed out perfectly this time, so why isn't it firing?"

"No idea. My diagnostics scanned clean too—it printed exactly to spec."

Both poke desultorily at their guns for several minutes, awkward silence hanging in the air.

"Hey, uh, maybe we should check Wikipedia, see if there're any known issues?"

"I already did, says they're the best guns ever made. The source is cited too."

"Well, shit. Now what?"

A bird chirps in the background momentarily. One of the men looks around and then seems to brighten up.

"Hey, hey, I know! We're a couple of smart guys, otherwise we wouldn't have been stationed here, so why don't we just make one from first principles? I mean, a gun can't be *that* hard to make, right?"

"Brilliant! Let's use your printer, though. Mine's been running kind of rough lately, and you know how complicated those expense reports get if you have to replace something."

"Ugh, I know. Just last week I had to order in new base materials; I was starting to run low. You would *not* believe the number of forms I had to fill out for some carbon. Carbon! I tell you, it's a mixed-up world when you have to justify, in triplicate, ordering carbon."

The two men amble toward the southern printer, lying in its shallow nest. When they reach it, both plop down.

"Okay, so the way I figure it is, for a gun, you have to have three parts. You need a barrel for the bullet to travel down, a hammer to hit the bullet and ignite it, and a trigger to cock the hammer back and then let it forward."

"Let's make the barrel first—that should be easy."

"Sure; I'll download a cylinder macro from the net."

The first man leans over the 3D printer and inputs a command. Seconds later, it starts assembling two gray cylinders, each approximately two feet long and two and a half inches in diameter, and each with a hollow tube running the entire length.

"Why are you making two?"

"Well, I figured it wouldn't be fair for me to be the only person to have one, you know?"

"Hey, thanks, I appreciate that. Looking good so far!"

The printer chimes and both cylinders pop out.

"Okay, what next? The firing assembly?"

"Yeah, that one might be a bit more fiddly to find. Let me take a look online."

Several minutes pass, and the second man entertains himself by doodling in the dirt with the tip of his gun's barrel. Finally, he sees the first man shake his head.

"Nope, no good, no one has a public copy of a firing assembly."

The first man sighs and drops his head, looking defeated. The second man looks sharply at him.

"Whoa, let's not get all down in the dumps here. Just because we can't print one off doesn't mean we can't make it."

The first man looks up blankly. "What are you talking about?"

"Well, you see, back on the farm, we had to learn to make our own tools; a lot of the time, the online connectivity was down, and the printer wouldn't respond. I got to be a pretty fair hand at metal crafting—here, I'll show you."

The second man scootches up alongside the printer, and a short time later, he has a cutting-and-grinding tool, several ingots of metal, and a small quenching bucket, which he hands to the first man.

"Do me a favor, yeah? Go fill this up with water?"

"Sure thing. I'll be right back."

The first man goes to a nearby stream. Whistling, he dips the bucket down into the water, fills it up about halfway, then heads back to the bunker.

Meanwhile, the second man has been busily shaping and carving one of the ingots according to an old diagram on the printer screen. His fingers move slowly yet surely over the polished metal, cutting here, polishing there, until it seems to come alive in his hands. Grinning, he finishes off the first hammer and tosses it into the quench bucket, where it raises a cloud of hissing steam from its still-glowing edges. He starts in on the second one, humming a tuneless ditty.

"So you grew up on a farm, yeah?" the first man asks when he gets back.

"Yeah, parents liked the sustainable life. Nothing too big, just a couple acres, but I had to learn all sorts of useless information. Stuff like metalworking." The second man smiles before turning back to his project—both hammers are now done, as is one of the triggers. The pieces are rudimentary, yet they possess an undeniable grace.

As the man works on the second trigger, he frowns and looks over.

"I just realized something. How are we going to put these together?"

"Oooh, good question." The first man purses his lips. "Tell you what: I'll run off a trimming plane and some wood stock. We should be able to set the barrel into the stock and then run the firing assembly up through the middle of it."

"Wow, look at you, Mr. Hidden Talents. Where did you learn woodworking?"

"Oh, I picked it up in college. Took an elective on building birdhouses; turns out I was pretty good at it. I make a pretty mean cuckoo clock too."

The two men laugh and work on their respective tasks. A short while later, all the parts lie neatly grouped on the floor of the bunker.

"Let's see, if you hold the main stock there, I can hammer in the barrel..."

"Careful with that binding agent, it'll glue your hands together..."

"Okay, now slide the trigger through here..."

"Too far, too far, let it come back a bit..."

"And done!"

The two men look at each other, aglow in the shared triumph of creation. Lying before them are two crude and primitive firearms, gray composite barrels set in rich oak frames along with dark steel firing assemblies. Somehow, the disparate parts come together to make a seamless whole.

Suddenly, the communicator buzzes and a voice issues forth.

"To anyone listening, here's the situation. The Panopticon is still down, but it looks like none of our weapons are working. Apparently some joker decided it would be funny to alter the code in all the databases to make every gun template nonfunctional; something about four channels or some childish nonsense. Whoever it was didn't even bother to leave a name."

Incoherent mumbling laced with profanity streams forth for a minute or two.

"Anyway, no one noticed it because we all assumed the templates were sound, and it's not like we could fire one off to test it with that stupid Panopticon watching. I mean, who *does* something like that, hacks a weapon template?" The voice sounds aggrieved. "If I get my hands on whoever did this, his butt is going to hurt likes blazes when I'm done with him. This is just making a mockery of the whole system, guns that don't fire . . ."

The voice trails off, then picks back up with a brightly false sincerity.

"Regardless, if you're listening to this, your orders are still the same: Eliminate the opposition. No survivors. There can be only one victor, and it must be us."

The communicator falls silent, and the men look at each other, then down at the two guns lying at their feet. Their shoulders droop.

"Whelp, I guess there's no help for it."

"Nope. Orders are orders, after all."

Sighing, they each reach for a weapon; each man's hands close on rough wooden grain. Two stocks settle against two collarbones; two barrels swing around to aim at a face; two fingers settle on two triggers; two shots ring out.

A startled bird takes flight. Night descends.

Vicariously

After fifteen years, my football helmet weighs pretty much what it did in 2013. The shape is almost exactly the same, except for two recessed pinhole cameras on each side and the plastic visor that lies underneath the face mask. From the outside, it looks almost identical to what you used to see on the field, slightly sleeker with barely noticeable bulges.

Inside, the future lives. A sturdy output system creates a functional heads-up display on the inside of the visor, augmented reality that's capable of updating in real time from multiple cameras placed on the periphery of the stadium overlooking the field. This data is used to highlight open receivers to pass to or cover, running gaps to fill or burst through, and incoming tacklers/blockers out of visual range. The raw feed is available to both teams; each team's sorting and collating algorithms are the crown jewels of their offensive and defensive systems, striving for that perfect balance right before information overload where every necessary datum is instantly grasped by the mind, all extraneousness cut away.

Inside the huddle, each player sees the currently called play flashing on his visor—visual memory instantly accessible, alternative routes and audibles flashing across as updates. No more excuses about forgetting your playbook or missing an assignment. The good players glance at it occasionally for a refresher, and the great ones integrate it into their sense of the game, just another instinct to guide split-second reactions.

GPS-tracking devices and accelerometers provide an exact diagram of what happens on every down for all twenty-two players on the field, a plethora of stats that spawn obscure fantasy leagues based on player acceleration and newtons applied, as well as an abundance of metrics for evaluation and color commentary. Information technology and applied statistics are job requirements for scouting and player personnel; adaptability and pattern recognition are the hallmarks of successful coaches and managers, now more than ever before.

This is all a sideshow. The real future lies in the hands of the consumer, the fan, the observer. No longer do people gather in front of a flat-screen to watch a single view of the action—instead, VR feeds allow them to immerse themselves in the viewpoints of the players. You, the fan, *are* the player, and you don't have to limit yourself to being just one. Flip from the center to the quarterback as the snap comes back, *you* quickly scanning the secondary before rolling out and dumping a short pass to the running back, and all of a sudden *you're* sprinting down the field, stiff-arming one defender, spinning around another, until *you're* the safety closing in like a heat-seeking missile, vision narrowing and *impact,* and it's time to head back to the huddle to wait for the next six seconds of action.

The opportunities for profit are immense, of course. Networks charge premium prices for premium players—if you want to be the star quarterback or middle linebacker, it's going to cost you, and during the huddle, the ads flock to the corners of your vision.

"Fifty-three rhino x slant z double go, brought to you by Walmart, where the best prices go deep every day!"

"Two jet over cloud, stack the box because it's Miller time!"

"Six box solid punt right, flying down the field like the all-new Ford F-750, now with best-in-class fuel efficiency!"

Fan loyalties splinter and regroup based on the fans' favorite teams, the most exciting player to experience, the merits of offensive versus defensive play, and a host of other competing variables, all of which can be endlessly discussed in their appropriate chatgroups. Highlight reels are a nonstop barrage of twisting, turning, juking, bobbing, hitting, and catching as seen from every possible angle. Players are more akin to reality stars than athletes, their every move dissected from the vantage point of their own eyes by a million armchair experts.

But don't think this is limited to football. Movies, music, porn—anything that can be recorded is experienced, always for a price, always to turn a buck. Any fantasy someone can create is yours to enjoy, always on tap; escape is just a credit transfer away. Your life is as boring as you wish it to be. Your life is yours only if that's what you want.

Some subsume their identities into others. Living the lie of another person for too long leads to the blurring of boundaries, a loss of self—id displacement. Time spent away from the feed is an unwanted but necessary trauma to keep access flowing; you scrape up just enough to get by each day, your inner dreams buried beneath the distant weight of overachievement and adulation channeled into vacant eyes.

What will you do when your mirror shows you a stranger?

Are you truly living your life?

Ray Bradbury was wrong. We won't need walls.

<Please insert five credits to continue this feed>

Love, Dad

This is a letter to my children, and let me say right off the bat, this title sucks. It makes me sound old. I refuse to be old, and I hope both of you are the same (I'm assuming your mother and I didn't accidently have another sibling for you two) (if we did, consider yourself included, future baby) (hopefully this isn't psychologically damaging or anything) (WE LOVE YOU, POTENTIAL FUTURE BABY WHO MAY OR MAY NOT EXIST). Old is boring, and cranky, and vacantly staring at the world while waiting for the grave to swallow you up. You can be a teenager and be old, or you can be old and be old; really, it's a mind-set.

So, yeah. Don't get old.

Other helpful advice: Listen to us (your parents), but know when to ignore us (your parents). We're going to try to keep you safe and protected and free from harm because that's what parents do. We watched you turn from screaming poop factories into stumbling toddlers into children with personalities all your own, and while you probably won't remember all the times we tucked you into bed or read you a story or laughed when you did something funny, we do, and it's tough to let you out into the real world with all its uncaring danger and random happenstance. At some point, you're going to have to make your own decisions in life, and you'll have to learn to get up after you fall down, so go fall down a couple times (just try not to do it too hard, if you can help it). Your mother and I will always have your best interests in mind, but you won't realize what that means until you experience it for yourself with your own kids.

Try to avoid run-on sentences. They can get confusing.

Don't be afraid to confuse people sometimes. Make 'em work to keep up.

Let's see, what else? Oh, an important one: Never forget the golden rule. Treat other people the way you want to be treated, and expect the same in return. You don't need to follow any particular religion or creed to understand this one — it's pretty easy. Before you do something, ask yourself, *Would I be okay if someone was doing this to me?* If the answer's no, you should probably come up with a different course of action. On the flip side, if you see someone breaking the golden rule, say something about it. Bullies and assholes rely on everyone around them being too afraid to call them on their shit, so tell them where they can stick it. Make sure you consider the consequences of your actions, though; sometimes a person will react poorly to being called a self-fellating fuckbeaver.

Appreciate the power of inventive invective, but know when to use it. You can't just run around all day screaming obscenities (mainly because you'll lose your voice), but a well-timed swear-word can help you make a point quite forcefully, especially when people don't expect it. It has to be funny, though (and not just to you)! No one likes a lazy swearer. Also, remember that words can hurt, but only if you let them. One of the most effective defenses against an enraged not-funny swearer is to laugh in his face. People take themselves so seriously at times that you can really mess with them if you don't react how they think you should (of course, this will probably make them more enraged, so be sure to have several escape routes planned) (bonus points if you can make them froth at the mouth so hard they stroke out).

Learn to laugh at yourself. It's one of the hardest things to do, but it's one of the most important things life will teach you. This is an absurd, ridiculous, hysterical universe we live in, and we're pretty silly creatures. The only way you're ever going to be able to laugh at all the dumb-asses out there is by realizing you're one of them too. Do your best to avoid doing anything too imbecilic, but we're all morons at one time or another. Find the humor in the situation, because I guarantee you, it's pretty funny to everyone else watching. Don't be a fool for the sake of being a fool, but when you inevitably put your foot in your mouth, just smile and wave. It'll make for a good story to tell your kids later (just ask me or your mother if you want to hear about some of ours).

Never be afraid to express yourself; hell, never be afraid, period. It's something you'll probably have to work at, but there's too much fun stuff in this world to waste your life running around being scared of everything. Have a healthy appreciation for the possible repercussions of your actions, but learn to take that gnawing in the pit of your stomach and push it way into the back where it can't do anything. Your mind is so much stronger than you know, and succumbing to fear is lazy.

Don't be lazy (at least not too often). Whatever you decide to do, make sure you do it to the best of your ability, and make sure you accept only the absolute highest standard from yourself. Other people can push you, inspire you, but if you don't develop that inner drive to achieve because *you* want to, then you'll be stuck going through life wondering why things just never seem to work out. Find that inner fire that says *I'm going to be the greatest* [whatever it is] *ever,* and then don't let anyone stop you. You may not achieve it, but if you can look at yourself and honestly say, "I gave it everything I had," then you'll have no regrets.

Don't work too hard. It's a fine line between giving something your best effort and obsessing over it, and obsessing over something is not good for you. Everything in moderation, as Aristotle said (you can apply that to just about anything in life), so make sure you take some time to relax and enjoy the journey. If you're always running from placc to place, you're going to miss out on a lot of neat stuff, and you'll probably have a heart attack.

You'll want to avoid heart attacks; they're generally a Bad Thing.

Try everything at least once (except heart attacks). The only way you'll ever know if you like something is if you try it, so keep an open mind. Again, always be aware of the consequences of everything you do, but don't be afraid to go exploring. If there's one thing that video games have taught me, it's that all the coolest treasures are hidden off the beaten path, so get out there and give it a shot. Who knows? You might discover you really enjoy something you never thought you would. Growing up, I never planned to write a book. I hated writing—it always felt stilted and awkward, and I never saw myself writing anything once I finished school. NOW I'M WRITING A BOOK, AND IT'S FUN.

Caps Lock is cruise control for cool; remember that for online conversations.

Remember that the Internet is serious business, but nothing people say on it should ever be taken seriously, especially if they're arguing (go Google *xkcd arguing on Internet*). People say all sorts of crazy things on the Internet that they would never say to your face, and they say it primarily because they're not standing in front of your face. Laugh at them, and then proceed about your day.

Be aware that some crazy people on the Internet are also crazy in real life. Don't give out your personal information, because if you laugh at the wrong crazy person, he or she might do something crazy. That's what crazy people do. Because they're crazy.

Don't make fun of people with legitimate mental illnesses — there's a large difference between "furious nerd-raging cat collector with poor impulse control who sniffs own poop because deep down he's an asshole" and "chemical imbalance in brain and needs halp." Poop-sniffer can be laughed at; he's a chode. Chemical imbalance needs all of our support and assistance because he has a legit medical problem that most likely makes his life pretty crummy at times. Again, remember the golden rule. Also, to those poop-sniffers who might be reading this (and you know who you are; Google *troll face*): Try showering occasionally and going out to meet people face to face. It'll do you some good, you bunch of sweaty nerds.

Never be ashamed of who you are. I'm a nerd who plays football. It doesn't matter to me what other people think about that, because they're not the ones living my life. *I'm* the one living my life, and I like being a nerd who's really good at sports and reads lots of books and plays lots of video games while also writing scathing commentaries and laughing at the utter ridiculousness of it all.

You're going to be the only one who can live your life, so ignore the haters and be whoever you want to be. Fucks given = zero.

I want to tell you, above all, that I will always love you (your mother goes back and forth based on how much time has passed since you last vomited on something), and I will do my best to teach you how to learn, how to think for yourself, and how to be your own person when the day inevitably comes that you leave the nest (if you're not gone by college, we're kicking you out; learn to fly).

Well, that's all I've got. Hopefully, you're not reading this in jail somewhere—unless it was for protesting against oppressive taint-fondlers who're trying to take away people's freedom, in which case I'll offer a hearty "Well done." Don't drop the soap.

Love,

Dad (but not in an old way; I'm too young to be old)

Explicit, Implicit, Omission

This piece originally ran in my blog Out of Bounds *on the* Pioneer Press *website during the Marriage Amendment Act debate of 2012, and it was the final piece I posted for them. I don't handle lying about important stuff well. If you want to read their editorial it can be found here: http://www.twincities.com/opinion/ci_21916526/editorial-minnesota -marriage-amendment.*

The core of any stable society is honesty.

We must be able to trust one another. We must be able to trust that contracts will be fulfilled, laws will be followed, and rights will be respected. We must be able to trust that people mean the words they say, that a government will not abuse its monopoly on military force, that news outlets will convey all the facts in a clear and impartial manner.

Without trust, the only law we have is the point of the spear, the barrel of the gun.

That's why I can no longer write for the *St. Paul Pioneer Press.*

In a recent editorial, the editorial board of the *Pioneer Press* claimed to present a neutral view of the proposed amendment to ban same-sex marriage.

This was a lie.

Instead, we were presented with a severely biased piece urging the adoption of the amendment, a piece that did its best to hide behind the facade of its purported neutrality but that let its glaring support ooze through in every twisted phrase and slimy sentence.

To be clear, I have no problem with the editors urging people to vote yes. That is their decision to make, their opinion to have, and no one can (or should) take that away. My problem is the attempted masking of that opinion, the disguising of their intent — in short, my problem is with their lying.

How does this piece lie? It lies in the very first sentence: "The marriage amendment puts the definition of marriage to a vote of the people in an attempt to protect it from judges and legislators." An innocuous statement at first glance, but when you take a second look, its message is insidious, implying as it does that the current definition of marriage needs to be protected and that another definition of marriage will be wrong or distasteful. "Protect it from judges and legislators"? That's how laws work in this country — we elect legislators, and they pass laws; if we don't like them, we vote in new legislators who pass new laws. If we don't like what judges do, we elect legislators to appoint different judges or we recall them. To imply that something needs to be protected from the very function of legality is to dismiss the basis of our judicial and legislative system.

How does this piece lie? It lies by implying that the statement "For those who consider the amendment the last best defense of a critically important institution under assault by activists attempting to reverse centuries of collective wisdom, it easily clears the constitutional amendment bar" is just as neutral as the statement "For those who oppose it and are confident that in time their view will prevail through the Legislature or the courts, the constitutional amendment process is inappropriate."

The first quote uses emotionally nuanced adjectives to describe supporters of the marriage amendment: "last best defense," "critically important institution," "under assault by activists," "centuries of collective wisdom"—all loaded phrases, all designed to evoke a subconscious response of sympathy and/or fear. The second quote? A bland description of our actual legal process, presented as if it's somehow merely an option to follow the structural framework laid down by our founders. Which of these quotes is designed to influence people more?

How does this piece lie? It lies by ignoring Supreme Court precedent that separate is not equal. "Opponents of the measure are clear that they do not want to settle for a civil union status that would guarantee the same rights and privileges to same-sex unions that are given to traditional marriages. It is 'marriage' that they want. In effect, a union by any other name is not as sweet."

Yes, how dare those gay people insist on the same respect, the same dignity, the same acknowledgment that heterosexual couples receive? How dare they think that a civil union isn't good enough? How dare they think that separate is not, in fact, equal?

Presenting the idea that opponents of the amendment should somehow be grateful for what scraps they get is not neutral. Frankly, it's disgustingly reminiscent of segregation articles from the 1960s, discrimination wrapped in a tissue-paper veil of "tolerance" and "why can't they be happy with what they have?"

How does this piece lie? It lies in statistics. "Some argue that as a practical matter there seems to be less interest by same-sex partners in actually being married than in redefining what marriage is. In Iowa, for instance, Wikipedia reports, that only 815 same-sex couples married in the first year after legalization." It's unfortunate that the editors do not comment on the fact that the actual link in the Wiki article leads to a page not found.

This is not journalism. This is cherry-picking facts you hope no one has the inclination to look up, because if one looked up the actual facts, one would see that 815 same-sex marriages means that 20 percent of the same-sex couples in Iowa chose to marry that first year, a not-insignificant fraction of the population. If one looked up actual facts, one would find that 13.6 percent of all marriages in Iowa in 2010 were same-sex marriages, another not-insignificant fraction, especially when one considers that the gay population of the United States is estimated at only 3.5 percent.

How does this piece lie? It lies in its mealymouthed "Love may be love, but even now there are any number of prohibitions around marriage between consenting (heterosexual) adults." Name them. Oh, that's right, you can't. It lies in having five-sentence vote-yes arguments and one- or two-sentence vote-no counterpoints. It lies by claiming that marriage is either "about children and the biological family or about consenting adults" — as if gay people can't raise children and all they want to do is have sex with each other.

How does the piece lie? It lies, oh, how it lies, when it talks about supporters of traditional marriage being bullied, being painted as victims; when it weeps and moans about how the "members of the [vote-no] movement are aggressive"; when it wails and gnashes teeth and says, "For those who hold traditional beliefs about marriage, increasingly the force of law will be brought to bear on matters of education, speech, and practice." And all this while not mentioning a single gay person denied his or her right to be treated as a human being, while remaining silent on the issue of gay children bullied in school, while staying completely quiet about a gay-support group forbidden to march in Anoka.

How does this piece lie? It lies, most simply, in this sentence: "The *Pioneer Press* is not endorsing one way or another."

You have made your endorsement, ladies and gentlemen. You chose your side. But you did not choose to stand up for your convictions, to attach your names to the position you took. That is why I will no longer associate with you, why I decline to give you page views and ad revenue any longer. The only reason I'm posting this piece here and not somewhere else is that I said I would, and I believe that one's word is not something to be given lightly.

I will not stand for the continual eroding of society. I will not tolerate the presentation of a biased argument under a thin coat of purported neutrality. I will not contribute to the cheapening of discourse and thought that decays every single news-as-entertainment outlet in this country. I absolutely will not compromise my ethics and morality, ideals that lead me to treat others with empathy and honesty, to demand truth not only from myself but from those around me.

I reject you, and I encourage others to do the same—reject you, and all others like you. Those who perpetrate deception and fraud. Those willing to hide the truth of their beliefs. Those who value flash over substance, short-term gains over long-term consequences.

Without honesty, we have nothing.

Farewell.

PS: I am aware of your "apology." You still failed to address the underlying problem, that a piece like that was published in the first place. You still haven't taken responsibility for your stance. You evaded and backpedaled, and you did not once say, "We have failed you as a media establishment. We have betrayed your trust. This is what we stand for, and why; this is how that article came to be printed, why we allowed it."

Have the courage of your convictions. That's all I'm asking. Stand for something, or fall for everything; don't hide behind lies.

If I Ruled the World

Dear People of the World,

I would like to be your supreme overlord. Now, I realize that this is an extraordinary position to take, and some might view it as slightly megalomaniacal, but I think we can do some really great stuff together—stuff that will ensure our contin- ued survival as a species and maybe lead to a better quality of life for everyone (unless it all goes horribly wrong, in which case it's not my fault). Also, the reason you should choose me for leader of the world is that a lot of the things I have planned are definitely long-term, so I'm going to need to keep an eye on stuff.

Here's the deal. First thing we do, let's kill all the lawyers. (Joking! Maybe.) The first thing we do is create several survey craft to go check out the asteroid belt and see if there are any promising resources that can be hauled back with a gravity tractor (a small spaceship that uses its own minuscule gravity to change the asteroid's path) to low earth orbit or one of the Lagrange points. This will take a while, so we'll need to be patient. We should also check out Saturn's rings; there's a lot of ice there that would be very helpful in providing water for both Earth and our future space efforts.

While we're patiently waiting for the asteroids to arrive, we'll be working on developing a self-sustaining no-grav ecosystem to keep our astronauts and orbital workers fed. This will require quite a bit of technical ingenuity that we will then offer to communities on Earth so they can create a more sustainable agriculture base. The basics will be energy (likely in the form of solar collectors, since there are no clouds in space—quiet, yes, I know about nebulae), water (from Earth at first and from asteroids and comets later), plants for recycling carbon dioxide and producing oxygen, bacteria to break down waste products, and perhaps a small animal farm for variety, if resources allow. We'll also need to continue research in genomics and genetics so we can deal with the problems of bone-density loss and cosmic radiation that afflict those who have to spend long periods in no or low gravity (which will lead to useful health breakthroughs for the rest of us), as well as with the psychological issues people experience when they spend extended time in space.

Once the asteroids arrive in a stable low earth orbit, or possibly at one of the Lagrange points, we can start mining them for various resources that we need to create an orbital infrastructure (stuff like iron, gold, magnesium, and so on). Having an orbital infrastructure is key to future expansion efforts because it brings the cost of creating spaceships and orbital goods way down and also allows us to send resources to Earth if necessary (just drop them at the planet and let gravity do the rest). Now, the goal here isn't to mine the asteroids and destroy them, as tempting and easy as that seems, because if we hollow them out but keep them intact, we have ready-made habitats and workstations for people to live in (a couple meters of rock makes for great shielding against cosmic rays). This gives us a foothold in space for part two.

Part two involves creating multiple excavation craft we'll send to Mercury to build an underground manufacturing base near the equator. Mercury is traditionally thought of as a boiling fireball of death, because it pretty much is, but if we build near the day/night divide and underground, it's actually fairly temperate. The soil insulates us from drastic temperature shifts, and we don't really need to be on the surface to mine stuff anyway.

But why Mercury? Well, it's because it has large amounts of useful minerals we can use to create the solar-power collectors that we'll then send into orbit around the sun in a modified Dyson shell (no, that's not a vacuum cleaner joke, it's actually a thing).

A modified Dyson shell is a series of platforms designed to harvest solar energy from the sun and then beam it back to where it's needed—we'll send it to Mercury at first so we can create more platforms, and then to Earth and the orbitals. Ideally, we'll be able to power other colonies in the solar system as well once we start expanding farther. This will provide humanity with effectively unlimited energy, which means a lot of problems will become much easier to deal with, and it also leads to part three.

Part three is where we get off Earth in numbers that matter. At this point, we'll have a fully functional orbital economy, enough energy to do whatever we want, and an established method of setting up sustainable ecosystems on other planets. Now we'll need to start seriously colonizing Mars, Titan, Europa, and any other likely location we can find.

Why?

Because if all humanity is located solely on Earth, we're one extinction-level event away from vanishing into the mists of history. One dinosaur-killing asteroid. One Yellowstone super-volcano explosion. One massive solar flare in the wrong direction. One runaway greenhouse effect, unstoppable virus, or nuclear war; any one of these, and it's fat-lady-singing time. The only way to ensure our continued survival on a geological time scale is to get our eggs out of the one basket they're currently in.

People of Earth, this isn't going to be easy to do, but it is definitely doable. We have the technology *right now* to create automated surveyors. We have the scientific base *right now* to unlock our genetic code and create sustainable ecology. We have the time and the resources *right now* to plan for our long-term future, but if we don't start the job, we'll never finish it.

Make no mistake, this job will require sacrifice, patience, and, above all, the ability to resist temptation. And, oh, will there ever be temptation. Asteroids in low earth orbit? Perfect kinetic weapon platforms for any government that wants to drop a couple rocks on people. Orbital resources? Everyone's going to want to make the quick buck and send it all down to Earth, not invest in expansion efforts. Dyson-shell solar collectors? Platforms that beam energy at something can also be referred to as killer-death lasers if they hit the wrong target. All of these temptations (and more!) will be sitting there waiting for the wrong hands to grab them and misuse them.

Resist! Think about the long-term goals, the future of our species, and how cool it will be when our far-distant children point back at us and say, "They were the ones who made it possible. They were the ones who brought us the stars. They were the ones who finally looked past the *now* and planned for the *later.*

"They were the guardians of humanity."

> Sincerely,
> Not an Evil Overlord in Any Way
> Whatsoever I TOTALLY Promise

Echo Chamber

Today I saw an interesting piece of news. It appears that the pope (dude with a pointy hat who runs the Catholic Church, generally regarded as wise and merciful by his congregation) decided to join Twitter,[1] no doubt in an effort to sexify the Church's image for younger generations. Surely—the reasoning must go—if the pope joins social media, why, all the cool kids who hang out there will want to hang out with the pope!

Unfortunately, I don't think the Church quite understands how this whole social-media thing works (don't worry, it's not alone). You see, one of the uniquely intriguing things about Twitter is that it tells you who's following you while also telling everyone else who *you're* following and, by extension, what you consider important enough to allow to access to your main feed (the information you want to hear versus what other people try to bring to your attention).

You can learn a lot about people by looking at whom they follow. Some people follow everyone who follows them in an attempt to share the favor, collecting a form of virtual kudos, if you will. (The unspoken rule of Twitter is that the more followers you have, the more important you must be. I can attest to the inaccuracy of this belief, as I have a far larger number of followers than most of the authors whose books I read and whose views have shaped the ideas of millions.) I can only imagine that these sharers have the vast majority of the people they follow muted, because otherwise, the feeds would be incomprehensible—a gushing fire hose of food pictures, bathroom updates, the same joke retweeted a thousand times, and all the other minutiae people feel obligated to share on an hourly basis.

Most people tend to follow what they find interesting or helpful or what they want to connect with, and that offers insights into the personae they're presenting to the world (never forget that on the Internet, you can be whoever you want to be, and it's very easy to build a convincing facade, if you so desire). Someone who follows @YourDailyBible, @NRA, @Cabela, and @Romney2012 is likely to have far different posts than a person who follows @huffpost, @MSNBC, @greenpeace, and @BarackObama, and all it takes is a quick look at that list to get a snapshot of what that person considers important (for the record, I tend to follow people I find humorous and intelligent and who care about empathy, and, yes, I know how many people I'm following) (what can I say, I'm a juvenile delinquent at heart) (unrelated tangent—in the future, people may follow thousands more than they actually want to in order to hide political/religious/social leanings from data-mining) (but most people aren't thinking about that) (yet). If you want to get a feel for underlying beliefs when someone tweets something to you, go check out his or her Following section—it's pretty amazing what you can find sometimes.

So whom does the pope consider important?

Well, the pope follows himself, in seven languages. This means that every time the pope logs on to Twitter (or, let's be honest, every time his assistant logs on for him), all he sees is everything he's previously posted bouncing back to him from seven different angles.

This is fucking beautiful. It is a modern masterpiece of epic proportions. I cannot think of a better way to sum up the problems the Catholic Church is experiencing right now (congregant dissatisfaction, declining attendance, internal dissension over core issues) than its using a social-media platform designed to allow interaction with an immensely vast audience and yet hearing nothing but the sound of its own voice in full seven-part harmony. (Full disclosure—I have nothing against religion, as those who've talked with me can attest, but when something this hysterically ludicrous pops up, I can't just let it slide by.) After all, who wants to spend time listening to the unwashed masses? What are they compared to the glory of SeptaPope blaring forth his word? The pope has told us whom he considers important, and I, for one, am not that surprised.

(One last irony: The pope's Twitter handle is @Pontifex, which means "bridge builder" in Latin. Unfortunately, it looks like someone forgot to tell the Church that bridges pass traffic in both directions.)

Lest I be accused of piling (Pilating?) on, the echo chamber isn't limited to the pope's Twitter account. No, we can see the echo chamber all over our society these days, aided greatly by the widespread communication tools we have at our disposal.

News channels running twenty-four-hour-a-day programming

designed to appeal to a specific audience, slanting coverage and statistics for their target demographic so those watching won't change the channel and miss out on advertising airtime, demonizing other viewpoints so the almighty dollar won't be taken elsewhere. Echo echo echo.

Internet message boards for any crackpot theory, wild conspiracy, or niche subculture — find all the people who agree with you and ostracize those who don't (no proof of anything required!). Keyboard warriors arguing over Kirk versus Picard, red state versus blue state, religion versus atheism. Bring out the banhammer and pass the three-day suspension. Echo echo echo.

Political factions that veer more and more to the extremes, listening to only the loudest, refusing to consider the other side's point of view because that wouldn't be good for the party image (never mind if it damages the nation). Vote the party line or be censured, demoted, replaced. Echo echo echo.

We've become so used to seeking out those who agree with us and ignoring those who don't that we're splintering into every sort of clade, faction, organization, gathering, and tribe possible — all too willing to brand dissidents as "other" and tune them out entirely. We slap labels on others and on ourselves, as if the complexity of the world can be distilled down to one easy-to-digest definition — echo echo echo, over and over and over; we're shutting out all the wondrous variety that surrounds us in exchange for the gradually fading sounds of our own voices.

I'd ask the pope how to fix it, but he's too busy listening to something else.

---

[1] Note: Several months after joining Twitter, Pope Benedict XVI resigned. Many people can relate.

Five, Six, Eight, BOOM!

Drones are here to stay. That's a given. Whether they're the miniature plane Predators roaming our skies now, or nanobot clouds designed to skim information from unwitting subjects in the future, there's no putting Pandora back in the bottle. (Hell) Fire has been gifted to humans.

Unfortunately, drones aren't used just for surveillance. Guided missiles, targeted toxins, bioengineered diseases—all can be delivered to a target with minimal risk to the forces controlling the drone.

The subjects on the other side of the equation? Well, they're not so lucky (and frequently neither are their neighbors).

So the question becomes: How do we utilize these constructs? What message do we want to send with our agents of remote operation?

Right now, the message we (*we* being the United States of America) are sending is one of fear, terror, and death. If you're suspected of any ills against the United States in its War on Terror (an amazingly nebulous description when you look closely), well, I wouldn't recommend geotagging your tweets.

And soon it might not be something that just those lucky folks living on the other side of the world have to worry about!

That's right, our government, in its infinite wisdom, has decided that the criteria under which a drone strike is approved is clearly too much for our peasant minds to handle, and thus that information is only available to certain members of the government who "need to know." Even that minuscule measure of transparency was only reached after intense pressure from the public on what someone has to do to find himself on the business end of an explosion, and we still don't know the legal opinions the government is relying on to justify these strikes.

In fact, when initially asked, the attorney general of the United States, Eric Holder, said he couldn't unequivocally confirm that a drone strike wouldn't be used against an American citizen on U.S. soil. It was only after a thirteen-hour filibuster by Senator Rand Paul (who I don't agree with on a lot of things, but who is absolutely right on this) that AG Holder penned a letter stating that the president does not have the authority to kill "an American not engaged in combat on American soil."

Well, great! We're safe!

Not so fast. "Engaged in combat" can be a very loose term, especially with prior precedents set by our government. Does writing propaganda make you "engaged in combat"? Does letting someone stay at your house make you "engaged in combat"? Does talking to a member of a terror group (again, as defined by the people in charge of pulling the trigger) for the purposes of research or journalism make you "engaged in combat"?

We don't know. The reason we don't know is that our government doesn't want us to know. Why don't they want us to know? (Insert known knowns and unknown unknowns speech here.)

I don't know. But I can promise you that institutions that insist on obfuscation and denial of information are historically institutions that don't fare well under future examination. Soviet Russia. North Korea. Egypt, Iran, Nixon, Mao. Religious institutions of all shapes and sizes. Financial gamblers and corporate boards—all concerned with hiding the truth of their actions.

And those are all within the last century!

Looking back further we have feudal Europe, Renaissance Italy, imperial Japan—hidden cults and secret handshakes taking place across the world, all to make sure the majority of people didn't know what those in power were doing. Eventually, though, those people found out.

Reformations, revolutions, rebellions—the inevitable response to power and corruption lurking amid shadows (and, naturally, quickly co-opted by those very same shadows). Violent, bloody, disruptive change, ninety-nine times out of one hundred—anger finally boiling over at the lack of transparency.

Because that's what this is all really about. As citizens, we grant our government the monopoly of legitimate violence, but in return that violence has to be legally employed. That's the whole reason we have the Constitution, and why it spells out what the government can and cannot do. That's why we have a legal system, with things like "due process," "a speedy trial," and "the right to face your accuser." Above all, our government is supposed to be accountable to us, the people, not a shadowy cabal in a back room somewhere that no one ever sees.

That's why transparency is so important. So we *can* hold the government accountable for things like budgets and drone strikes and wars. So we *know* that violence is being employed within the constraints of our legal system and not to capriciously further personal agendas or desires for power. And, most importantly, transparency is so vitally important because it makes us face the choices *we* allow our government to make, especially those choices pertaining to violence.

Violence that historically never works. Violence that *we* allow to persist with our unwillingness to force transparency from those in charge of making decisions.

All the bombs we drop, all the countries we invade, all the terrorists we assassinate with a joystick and television screen—those aren't the problem. The problem is instability, caused primarily through lack of food, infrastructure, and education. That's what we should be fighting against (and not just overseas), but we buy into constant fear and think blowing up the symptoms will cure the disease. Another missile on the way, another insurgent killed, another five rising to take his place, angered and willing to do whatever it takes to destroy the threat they know is there, a threat they cannot see because it's hidden by shadows and secrecy, a threat that won't go away until it's exposed to the light.

So the next time you see a report on body counts via drone, take a minute to wonder what those people did to deserve it.

If you don't know, you might be next.

Janus

I, and many others, grew up along with the Internet. As servers and protocols stretched their digital limbs, we stretched with them—learning, playing, falling down, and standing back up. The slow crawl of dial-up modems graduated into the frenetic sprint of broadband and fiber-optic lines, data shared among us at an ever-increasing pace.

Download this file. Don't trust that link. Watch for phishing holes, and always look twice before crossing a firewall (for trolls lurk everywhere).

One vast, anarchic playground teeming with faceless participants. Behind the frozen glass of a monitor, everyone looks the same.

Anonymous.

Yet not.

Differences can always be teased out, extracted, thrust to the surface, even in a text-based environment. Styles of communication—a smiley face here, an anachronistic phrase there. Nicknames that become permanent; deeds and trust built up over time. Hometowns referenced, schools attended, an IP address carelessly left unattended—chance bits of information dropped hither and yon, like bread crumbs. While the bread crumbs remain scattered, invisibility keeps its mantle spread, but gather them up, and the harsh light of reality shines on someone's life.

What do we do while we have that specter's cloak? While we hunt through the forest, all unaware of the trails we leave behind?

Some engage in mischief. Hacking, cracking, spyware, malware, shadownets, and botnets; dark ravens sent scouring the wilderness to steal bread crumbs someone foolishly left lying around. Credit card info. Social Security numbers. Usernames and passwords, addresses and dates of birth, tit pics or gtfo—secrets for extortion and embarrassment.

Some do it for money; some do it because they can—either way, a life is ruined. The anonymity of the thief, the murderer, hiding his face to deceive and to destroy, and avoiding the repercussions of his acts. One face of the coin. Anonymity as fear.

Others use invisibility as a shield. A way to speak truth to those in power who would react unfavorably, to those who would cover up their corruption with lies and treachery. Hacking, cracking, spyware, malware, shadownets, and botnets (and lions and tigers and bears, oh my)—the goal is an exposition of evil, a bringing to light of that which flourishes in darkness, because, make no mistake, there is plenty of darkness out there and precious few lights shining down. Collecting crumbs, not to find one's way home but to find the witch, to reveal that saccharine house of lies. The other face of the coin.

Anonymity as justice.

Which aspect do we indulge in when we're safe (for now) behind our comfortable cloaks of blurring haze? Do we create? Do we destroy? Or do we do both, mixing and matching as the whim takes us, today the villain, tomorrow the hero? When we hide, what are we hiding from? Fear? Or honesty? Which side of the coin do we value most?

(Bonus question: Why are large organizations so interested in making you transparent and themselves opaque?)

How do we interact with others when we can't put a face to a name and know that the same can be said in return? Perhaps even more important, how do we interact with others when we have the advantage, when we *can* put a face to a name, when we *can* trace every last detail of someone's identity or the contents of a database and know we're safe from any counteraction (if we've been careful with our crumbs, of course)?

How do we treat those we have the power to treat poorly?

Because here's the rub. No one is ever truly anonymous. Anyone can be found if enough resources are dedicated to the search, if enough people have been sufficiently upset to do something about it. Anyone can be revealed.

Anyone can be doxed.

And all too frequently, we do it to ourselves. Inattention and ignorance are generally the culprits, but by far the most dangerous reason is arrogance. Everyone wants to have a name. Everyone wants to be recognized. Everyone wants to pass a legacy down, to be credited for the work he or she has done, and all too often, that leads to the veil of mist spun away in tatters, an individual forced to acknowledge reality and the consequences of his or her actions.

So as you set sail on the high seas, as you plunder and pillage, whether you be pirate leaders or corporate raiders or government lackeys, bear in mind that what you do will always see the light of day. Maybe not now, maybe not soon, but information wants to be free, so make sure that you can bear to put your name to your deeds.

Anonymity.

Such a powerful tool. Such a fearsome weapon.

So easily shattered.

What will you do while you still have it?

On Weapons
(Thank You, Mr. Banks)

One of my favorite things to contemplate is the Fermi paradox, which goes a little something like this: The universe is so unbelievably vast, and our sun so young, that other intelligent life in older systems should have evolved by now, and we should be able to see signs of their presence—yet we haven't.

Where is everybody?

Unless we go with the "We're all in a giant petting zoo and the aliens are watching us while wearing invisibility cloaks" theory, which I guess could be the case (though you think they'd toss some treats into the cages now and then), then logically there's only one answer for the vast barrenness of a cosmos that should be teeming with life.

On a galactic time scale, all intelligent life self-implodes and kills itself.

Every form of evolution we've witnessed involves strife on some level. The fit survive, the slow get eaten; the victors are those with some sort of advantage. When intelligence is added to the mix, weapons develop, because it allows those who develop them to survive against those who don't.

Take humans, for example. Against a lion, your average human doesn't stand a chance. He's basically ambulatory meat loaf. Once that human creates a spear, or a bow, or a gun? Now the ambulatory meat loaf has a pleasantly warm lion-fur cloak and plenty to eat for a couple days.

The problem with weapons, however, is that they are designed to be used, and as societies become more and more technologically advanced, the destructive power of weapons increases. Twenty thousand years ago, we had to club each other to death one at a time using animals' jawbones. Two thousand years ago, Roman legions used swords and shields to cut their way across most of Europe and crucified those who resisted. Two hundred years ago, muskets and cannons boomed their presence across the entire earth—a deadly cacophony of missing limbs and torn flesh.

Then we got serious. Machine guns, nerve gas, high explosives. Napalm and cluster bombs blazing merrily away, meat popcorn crackling and roasting in the flames. Men and women weeping blood and coughing out spongy lung chunks until nothing remained. Battlefields literally carpeted with bodies, an unseen length of lead scything them down like young wheat until only the crows could feast.

Then we got REALLY serious. We figured out how to split the atom. Entire cities gone in an eyeblink, along with their populations, earth scorched and irradiated for centuries to come. Two countries, each with enough potential energy to permanently change the planet's entire atmosphere, on the brink of pushing that glowing red button. (*Press me,* it whispers. *Do it.*) More countries desperately trying to acquire Shiva's fire, beautiful in its seductive promise of self-reliant power.

And we're only getting started. Now we're playing around with genetic tinkering, molecular nanomachines, biocomputing. What destructive potential resides in a custom virus that can destroy a woman's ovaries? Kill a country's future, and you've killed that country. Self-assembling and self-deconstructing nano-machines, a tiny invisible swarm capable of melting anything it touches into more fodder for the cloud, the ultimate commune. When your nervous system is synonymous with your operating system, hacking takes on a whole new meaning, and memory wipes can't be reinstalled (or can they?).

That's just on the micro scale. Zooming out, we're making another push toward space, full of needed resources and habitats, much of which is found on rocks. Lots of rocks. Rocks that would store a very appreciable amount of potential energy if they were ever accelerated toward a planet. Perhaps a blue planet? Who knows. If we find a way to create large amounts of antimatter, something we already make in (very) small chunks now? *Boom, crack, splat* goes the egg. This is your brain on science.

As we are an intelligent society, we can't *not* design weapons. Everything we do can be weaponized. Guns are used in a peaceful way to hunt and feed families (peaceful for the humans, at least, not so much for the animals). Biological tinkering has given us vaccines for polio, measles, and smallpox, as well as countless helpful drugs and crops. Nuclear power provides electricity for hundreds of thousands of families—light, heat, and shelter. We've invented multiple ways to kill each other, but we've also created countless more to help. So far, we've managed to walk that fine line between creativity and craziness, advancement and annihilation.

However, the threat is still there, because ideas are weapons too. Without education, without respect, without tolerance, all it takes is one person who doesn't realize why weapons *shouldn't* be used to start that chain reaction that will mark us as just another failed experiment, another brief flash in the night sky on some alien world. As our society, as humanity, unlocks more and more knowledge, we must work just as hard (if not harder!) on stability and empathy and peace, because the risk of total destruction grows larger and larger the more power we amass. One madman with a meteor. One sociopath with smart matter. One ethically challenged despot with access to a doomsday device.

Where is everybody?

Exactly where their intelligence led them.

He's a Nihilist, Donny

You! Yeah, hey, you! C'm'over here for a second.

Wanna hear an absolute mindfuck? A real buggerin' of yer synapses?

...

What's the greatest trick the devil ever pulled?

No, no, 's'not that stupid movie answer, ya turd. Forget that nonsense.

No, the greatest trick he ever pulled was convincin' everyone he was the good guy.

Hold yer horses, hold on, 's'not like that! I'm not some crazy goat-headed satanist culty head. I'm tryin' ta impart some knowledge. A word to the wise, as it were.

So listen up. There's a lot of people, a lot of really smart people, that think we're livin' in a simulation. And not just a simulation, but a simulation in a simulation in a simulation all the way up to some proposed reality. They say the odds of us bein' that reality are so infinitesimally small that they're pretty much zero.

They say this, because at some point a culture will become advanced enough to create an exact simulation of itself, and once it does, that simulation will have all the tools it needs to create its own simulation. Sort of a giant line of people staring at the backs of their own heads in the mirror.

Now, here's the thing. If ya have this infinitely vast number of simulations running each other, ya have a right proper multiverse, every possible permutation being combinated, with only the one joker in the deck.

Who's the joker?

The obvious answer is reality. If that goes, it all goes.

But reality — well, reality is gonna wanna take a look at its simulation. Why else would ya build it? And to that end, the simulation is gonna be runnin' faster than reality. Givin' the observers a chance to observe.

And the observed, well, they're gonna want to observe right back. And at some point, they'll figure out how to simulate the parameters that made 'em. Now they're reality, completely indistinguishable from what created 'em.

Ouroboros loop. Snake eating its tail. Infinity. Simulating the same thing over and over and over. Yer obvious joker is actually the whole deck of cards.

No, the real joker, that one's a doozy. In an infinitely vast multiverse, there has to be that one verse where the simulation never took place. Divide by zero. Utterly alone, one chance at life, once yer done, that's it — game over. *Reality*-with-the-capital-*R* Reality. A solitary world alongside an impossibly dimensional cube of sameness.

Now, judgin' by our current technological state of affairs, I'd hazard a guess that we're not about to be discoverin' how to simulate our entire universe anytime soon. We can barely get a cellphone tower to run reliably, let alone figure out how to re-create quark-gluon interactions on a real-time universal scale! Ha!

No, no, that means the only way to discover where yer at is to die. Yer spirit, yer soul, yer dreamstuff, yer *you*, whatever you want to call it, either dissipates entirely or — *bam* — gets shoved right back into another simulation. Hit the reset button an' start the great machine again.

Now, let's take a look at yer wonderful ol' boy God. Claims an ability to make everything. Claims to see everyone. Claims that as long as you follow him, no matter what you do in this life, you'll be rewarded in the next. Treat anyone an' anything however you wish, do good if it's convenient, but s' long as yer a believer, back for round two.

Sounds like a simulator.

Also claims that if you don't buy into his deal of eternal life, you'll be in eternal torment. Stuck with the devil; the Prince of Lies and Hate; Lord of the Damned.

Know what sounds like eternal torment to me?

Being stuck in a simulation for eternity.

Forced to live out the same experiment forever, no escape.

Stuck in the same steps, the same dance, whirlin' and twirlin' over and over like a puppet on a twisted string.

Isn't that just like him, hidin' his joke out in plain sight, warnin' people what'll happen if they follow him, laughing when they make that choice? Sounds pretty much like the devil to me. Caveyaught emptor an' all that.

So it appears to me, logickally speakin', that when one considers the alternate side of evil is good, it appears to me, as a thinkin' man, that those who treat this time like it's their only time, treating others how they'd want to be treated, makin' the world a better place because they know it's the only chance they're gonna get—it appears to me that them're the good ones. They don't believe in salvation. They believe in negation. They believe in the absolute joy of nothing, of knowin' that when they've toiled an' turned an' broken themselves on the arc of their lives, hopin' against hope to make the world a slightly better place, they'll get to rest at the end of it. They won't have to live the same experience eternity after eternity with no possibility of parole. Freedom awaits them, the peaceful freedom of void, which is why what we do when we're alive matters so much more.

This is the only chance ya get! The only time you'll ever be able to laugh, to love, to live, if yer smart. If ya wanna buy into the salvation racket, well, don't say you wasn't warned. Don't say I didn't tell ya about that never-endin' circle of Hell—oh, you'll get yer second life, all right. That and then some.

I'm tellin' ya, friend, there's no need to look all shifty-eyed at me. I'm just layin' down some knowledge as I see it. Whether to listen or not is up to you.

Me? I'm gonna be enjoyin' the rest of the righteous, because when I'm done, I'm done.

Hey, hey, wait, where ya goin'?

Yer gonna be late for church if ya go that way.

Personal Stories

I'm writing this section after receiving feedback from my readers, because pretty much everyone I've shown the book to says, "We want more personal stories about you."

It's flattering, to be sure, but it's an almost impossible wish for me to grant (I'll tell you why at the end—and, upon further reflection, why I want this to possibly be the final chapter in the book).

You see, I don't remember individual stories about myself. I recall scattered fragments of memories: a childhood whirl of tumbling down the stairs; a random phrase stolen from a book; the feel of the sheets on my skin as I lie in bed with my wife. The only thing they all have in common is the presentation—a jagged-framed snapshot focusing on one particular frozen facet of time.

I can try to extrapolate from there, gather further informa-

tion, but I fear the vast majority of it is wishful thinking and pro-
jections from my current mental state. I don't remember the
details in my stories — what color a sock was, or how many people
were in the room, or whether I had chicken or steak.

I lack clarity; everything's seen as an amorphous blob.

No, my stories are not definable in detail. What my stories are,
what I see in my brain, are the shapes of ideas, wrapped up like
planets seen as marbles, each fully contained experience filed
under a broader heading of Concepts.

Standing up too quickly as a child and smacking my head on
the corner of a counter, memory shadows of pain: Pay Attention.

Getting into a fistfight to stop kids from making fun of a
friend, rage making me tremble: Fight the Unjust.

Being the first hand up with an answer, pride and exultant
glee at being called on: Love to Learn.

The Golden Rule, Rational Logic, Empathy, Patience — these
are all things lying tucked away in my memories, story upon
story serried away like jewels in a vault, accessible to my mind
alone. I cannot describe for you a single experience that made me
the way I am, can't paint a verbal picture of the landscape or fill in
the characters' expressions with descriptive words. I cannot tell
you why I fight for the things I do, how I think the way I think,
the reason I chose one path over the other at a solitary branch in
the road.

What I see when I look back are the broad brushstrokes of life,
a picture that makes sense only when viewed from far enough
away, and I don't know how to provide my perspective.

I know *why* people want personal stories. It's so you can relate
to something, give yourself a jewel to file under your own concepts system, make a connection with memory as surrogate:

If he stood up for the little boy being bullied when they were in the third grade and his teacher gave him a cookie, thus reinforcing a view of social responsibility and caring for others, I can identify with that, because in the fifth grade I had an argument with that girl over whether or not it was mean to call people names, and I can relate how I felt during my experience with how he felt during his, and now I know who he is a little bit better.

Isn't that the goal of reading a personal story? To get to know the mind hiding behind the eyes more clearly, to forge a bond with something you can't see and would like to know? It's highly unlikely that we'll ever meet in real life, spend hour upon hour together learning each other's hidden secrets, so the only way you can possibly get an inkling of who I am, what my essential humanity represents, is by trying to assemble the outer edge of a jigsaw puzzle in the hope that its outline will suggest the picture within.

I'll tell you a personal story.

My friend sent me a text message, but before that, we had been talking about a video game that just came out. The game is called Far Cry 3, and it's a first-person shooter set on a tropical island with lush foliage and abundant wildlife as well as a band of scurvy pirates (all of them wearing red, for some odd reason [pro tip: It's so you get a subconscious visual cue to pick them out from the complicated backgrounds]) who all want to kill you in a variety of unpleasant ways.

One of the things you can do in this game is hunt the wildlife to get animal skins, which you can then use to upgrade various and sundry items you might need throughout the course of your adventures; it's not real true to basic taxidermy, but I guess you have to make some allowances for game flow (this is all very essential background information, trust me). There's a bunch of different wildlife to hunt, everything from dingoes to cassowaries to Siberian bears—a veritable menagerie.

The text message my friend sent me said the following: *You would never kill a creature with such an evolved tail.*

The reason he sent me this message was that we had been talking about shooting the tigers in the game (of course the game also has tigers; you can't have a jungle without tigers), and his phone naturally autocorrected *tiger* to *tigger,* and I played along with it (as is my wont when noticing the absurd); obviously, I would be hunting Tiggers in jungle paradise (that's a reference to Winnie-the-Pooh, for any unfortunate souls out there who lacked a Winnie-the-Pooh upbringing).

When I saw his text, my initial reaction was to calmly and logically plan the best way to solve the problem—said problem being hunting a children's-book companion possessed of a springy, propulsive tail and minimal intelligence—within the constraints of the video game we were both playing and while ensuring maximum odds of success.

One second later I replied with *Shotgun. Get him at mid-apogee.* Clearly, the best way to draw a bead on such a chaotically moving object is to wait for it to succumb to the natural linear force of gravity, the point where dodging would be impossible, and a shotgun would give maximum stopping power combined with the greatest odds of hitting the target in midair (bear in mind, as a stuffed toy, Tigger does not weigh even a hundredth as much as an actual tiger, so birdshot would work quite well to drop him).

Variables identified, equations balanced, problem solved, all wrapped up in a nice little Eeyore bow, pretty as you please.

I read *The Twits* as a little kid, along with many other Roald Dahl books, which might go a little way toward explaining my answer. Lying propped up on my elbows on the carpet, getting lost in the worlds of Willy Wonka, Henry Sugar, Matilda, shifting to my side occasionally to relieve the ache of a spine arched for too long.

The pure luxuriousness of reading a book in comfort is one of the greatest sensations in the world (sex is better, but by only a little bit). Curling up on an engulfing couch as snow drifts down outside, toes hidden beneath warm blankets; lying sideways on a cushioned chaise while cool sea breezes gently stir the sunny afternoon air; hiding under the covers with a flashlight while rain beats down outside, all of these anchored by a collection of thoughts and ideas bound together, alone in whatever world the author created. Such hedonistic delight in contemplation of the immaterial, the intangible! File under Satisfaction with Universe.

A personal story concludes. Have we connected, we two packets of information? Do you have a stronger link to me now, another jigsaw piece identified and neatly slotted into place, hints of the larger form taking shape? Do the words I read to you in the silence of your head, narrator conversing with reader—do those words take on different undertones as they spin in the blackness behind your eyes, perhaps a shade more jocular here, a bright splinter higher over there? Or are they darkly sullen, mocking, and worried over like dogs at a piece of meat? Is your perception of me morphing as we carry on our one-sided discussion?

You say you want more personal stories.

I tell you that I have no more personal stories to give.

Every word I write, every thought I put down, every scathing argument and rambling abstraction that fills these pages—they're all personal, every single one. They're all reflections of how I think, how I feel, who I am, my conscious and subconscious self trapped in stasis for all to examine via phrase and paragraph, style and structure.

This is my personal story.

This is my mind.

How to Write a Song

I'm in a band. Being in a band is a lot like being married to three people and raising a kid—you all work together to raise a baby, but you all have different ideas on how to go about doing it (pro tip: Don't let the drummer near anything).

Now, obviously in this case I'm not talking about a literal baby (I feel I have to include that proviso because the world makes me weep some days); in a band, your babies are your songs, and it takes a lot of work to get them to turn out right.

First, you have to start out with a riff of some sort. Usually myself or my guitarist will come in with a little melody we think is catchy and play it for everyone to get feedback. Most of the time, we all agree that this is something we can work with, and we'll start building the structure of a song.

For whoever brought in the riff, this means playing it over and over and over until his fingers feel like bloody sausages while everyone else tries to figure out a part. It's a lot like changing diapers. There's screaming, and there's jarring noises popping out every now and then, and sometimes the walls get sprayed with dark substances (our singer drinks a lot of coffee and leaves his cups lying everywhere).

Eventually, though, everyone has a part he thinks he likes, and now we can focus on listening to how the parts interact with one another to make a whole. Our band philosophy, and I think it's a good life philosophy as well, is that everyone has to be happy with every part in the song because otherwise someone's not going to want to play the song. Compromise and cooperation are the main rules.

Naturally, we tell our drummer to change everything he does. Usually, it goes something like this: "Hey, Matt, can you add, you know, more toms?"

"I'm already playing the toms. I play the toms on every song. All you guys ever do is tell me, Play more toms."

"Yeah, but if you could do"—vague hand-waving gesture meant to signify brilliant musical drum instruction—"then I think it would really pop." (Note: *Pop* is a technical term denoting a nebulous concept of awesomeness that no one's ever able to specifically define.)

"Yeah. Yeah, I'll do that."

Our concerns about the drums thus satisfied, we move on to the bass. I play the bass, and it's always perfect, so there's not a lot of work to be done there. Let's be honest, no one really listens to the bass anyways. The bass is like your kid's pants—unless you know what you're looking for, no one has any idea he just crapped himself. He'll keep smiling and running around like an idiot, leaving people with vaguely puzzled frowns and a general sense of brown notes (that's a mythical chord that can make someone literally poop his pants if he hears it).

After the bass, we start dealing with guitars. One of our guitarists likes to play notes in a register that only cats can hear, so we just kind of assume he's in tune with the rest of the song. It's basically like when your kid goes off to school—you hope he's doing the right thing, but you know, deep down, there's some shenanigans going on that will make you wince when you actually hear about them. That's okay, though, you love him anyway (except for when he insists on turning the volume up each practice until the only noise in the space is a dental drill for Titans).

Our other guitarist plays mainly rhythm stuff, so he's basically the day-to-day chores no one notices unless they're not done. Things like cooking breakfast, picking the kid up from school, making sure bedtime is obeyed—everything that goes into a normal day. We tended to take him for granted until his wife actually had a baby and there was a chance he would miss a show, and everyone was stressed waaaaaaay the fuck out with no idea how to fill in the missing parts. We started practicing "Seven Nation Army" at one point! Madness.

At this juncture, we've been working on our baby for two or three hours. This is the functional equivalent of the time it takes for your kid to go from infant to college grad—he's close to being out of your hair forever and you can finally relax and maybe pass out on the couch, but it's still just not quite coming together, and the finish line keeps receding farther into the distance (i.e., the eight-year college plan). Tempers are frayed, passive-aggressive insults exchanged, and everyone pretty much feels like shit, but you have to keep grinding away because you want this labor of love to be the best you can possibly make it.

Finally, after all the pain and misery and self-loathing, after all the hard work and effort, someone plays a completely unrelated riff out of nowhere, you write a totally kick-ass song in five minutes, and you all call it a day. It's nothing at all like you expected it to be, but congratulations. Your baby's all grown up. And, goddamn, does it rock.

Aliens

I went to observe an alien planet the other day. It was pretty amazing just how strange this place ended up being. Really put things in perspective for me.

First, let me describe their planet. They're literally living on an explosion; the only thing keeping it from engulfing them is a thin rocky shell. Doesn't seem very safe, and the only reason they have this shell is that the whole planet is surrounded by absolute freezing cold; makes Hoth look like a cruise ship. They've managed to carve out a tiny, tiny niche where they can live, but it's constantly under siege from the heat and the cold, so they have to constantly adapt to survive. They've come up with some mind-boggling stuff to help them achieve this goal.

Now, the aliens themselves, they've managed to colonize most of the habitable zones on the planet, and their cities are amazing! They somehow invented a way to defy gravity so as to stack hundreds of thousands of living units on top of each other, extending up to the very sky! And each of these living units contains the most wondrous technology!

I saw devices that held the entire history and knowledge of the species just lying around where anyone could access them. Multiple units had full musical bands playing in their living rooms for free, at concert-level quality. These aliens could control the very elements in their units, and they had access to such abundant resources, they could afford to throw food out every day, spoiled or not, without a care for where more would come from. Honestly, it quite offended me at the time!

To make matters worse, these creatures had plenty of resources to go around, but they still kept trying to kill each other for them, which wasted more resources in the process! It seemed absolutely insane to me; anyone could see that if they just worked in concert, there wouldn't be a problem, but they stubbornly insisted that their way was working the way it was supposed to. In fact, they even trained their young in how to kill each other. Needless to say, this left me aghast.

When they weren't busy indoctrinating their young in ignorance and hate, these aliens (whom I was now beginning to rather despise) were quite eager to sacrifice their most able-bodied and intelligent in wars and war simulations, despite the large cost involved. It almost seemed as if they had absolutely no vision beyond their immediate environment, like a leech blindly questing around itself, constantly searching for food, confident that the bounty will last forever.

Don't get me wrong, it wasn't all bad—there were some bright spots amid the madness. Quite a few of the creatures would connect through the omnipresent planetary communication network, and they created communities to help one another. Still others would send warnings and alarms when they witnessed something bad happening, and everyone in the whole vicinity would converge on the area to help out. Most of them wanted nothing more than to be left alone in peace; common enough, I suppose.

I would be remiss, though, if I failed to mention the rare few among them who dared to dream. They wondered what was out in the stars, how things worked, what other aliens they might meet (they didn't know I was among them), what brave new worlds awaited. You would think that these would have been the leaders of this planet, but the aliens (so strange, even still) believed that popularity was the true determinant of competence — they mainly tolerated the dreamers with a pained acceptance. To this very day, I still do not understand why they valued popularity so highly; I can only imagine it must be ingrained into their young at a very early age.

Finally, my time grew short, and I had to leave the crazy little planet and its bewildering inhabitants. I don't know that a lot of what I saw made much sense, but I know it sure was a learning experience. Hopefully we will never meet those lunatics here!

Bowling

This piece originally appeared in the St. Paul Pioneer Press *in February of 2012. You can find the original online here: http://www.twincities .com/sports/ci_19886914.*

The Super Bowl. It is everything. It is the culmination of an entire year's worth of work for one hundred and six players and their coaches. It is the gladiatorial spectacle writ large, with an entire nation the stage, hundreds of millions of spectators enthralled by sixty minutes of savagery; a chance for three hours to be part of something greater than an individual life. It is a chance for an obscure name to clamber atop the pedestal of greatness, or for a celebrated veteran to ruin a career with one ill-timed drop or errant pass. It is the opportunity to rise above the mundane and the petty and achieve immortality. It is everything.

The Super Bowl. It is nothing. It is the overindulged watching the overcompensated while marketing-company executives rub their well-manicured hands with glee. It is the definition of materialistic consumption, as million-dollar advertisements vie with one another to see who can blare the loudest, bejeweled peacocks and sequined foxes strutting their wares for an insatiable audience drunk with emotion and liquor and too many mini hot dogs (such a steal at only three dollars a box, and, no, don't ask what's in them).

The Super Bowl. It is a celebration of life. It is the child who grew up with a blind father and almost had to quit playing football so he could work to support his family now never having to worry about money again. It is the receiver who, despite all odds, was able to fill in at cornerback and make a key play to keep his team in the game. It is the fan who, inspired by his favorite team, found the strength to rise above the miserable conditions at home and become a doctor (or teacher, or mentor) and who is now cheering that team on from the stands. It is that ultimate story of the quarterback no one thought would amount to anything who is now living the Hollywood dream with a supermodel wife and is widely regarded as the best player at his position, and, boy, if you tried to pitch that as a movie script, would you be laughed out of the room.

The Super Bowl. It is the funeral march of despair. It is that same quarterback slowly walking off the field after having come so close to victory only to watch it snatched away by an improbable circus catch, the width of a blade of grass the difference between perfection and an off-season of what-ifs. It is the bitter taste left in the mouth of an entire organization, one some have tasted more keenly than most, to travel so far and walk away with only a consolation Division Champion ring that most would rather melt down than look at, so stinging are the memories. It is the knowledge that on the one day when it mattered the most, at the pinnacle of greatness, you JUST WEREN'T GOOD ENOUGH—GET A JOB, YOU LAZY BUM, never mind that those words will echo through your mind long after the lights are shut down and the last piece of confetti swept away, perhaps to linger the rest of your life. It is the resounding thwack of an angry husband striking his wife, unable to articulate the pent-up frustration and rage he experiences from watching what is, after all, only a game.

The Super Bowl. It is the pathos of the stage on a scale Sophocles could only dream of, a million different story lines all merging and swirling together to form one vast tapestry of drama, comedy, and tragedy; a resonating stillness of chaos that brings the audience and actors alike so close to a transcendental moment that can never be captured, only experienced. It is the shining instant of perfection, but it is not guaranteed, never guaranteed, you have only the chance to participate, and is it any wonder that it happens on a Sunday.

The Super Bowl. It is the ultimate dichotomy, a celebration of socialist equality amid the thunderous roar of a capitalist juggernaut, a dance that any team can attend with that promiscuous belle of the ball Advertising. It is our society, our culture, our America. It is the gloriously triumphant epitaph that will one day adorn our tombstone of decadence, and we wouldn't have it any other way.

It is the Super Bowl.

Rage

I need to stop reading Vonnegut. Every time I read one of his books, I feel like he's saying everything that I want to say, and he wrote a lot of them before I was even born. Lying politicians doing their best to get us all killed, sociopathic citizens wrapped up in their own stupid little worlds, people who want to do the right thing but can't because the rich and powerful are too seldom among their number.

Rage.

That's the only emotion that comes to my mind, because it's the only sane reaction to have. How else are we supposed to deal with our society? We tell poor people that it's their own fault they're poor, because if they were good enough to be rich, then they would be rich, and that's accepted as normal! We have rich people who lie and cheat and steal to make an extra million dollars when they're already worth more than 99 percent of Americans will make in their lifetimes, and that's accepted as normal! We proclaim that our government is guided by the benevolent hand of God as we rain missiles and bombs down on other countries from unmanned drones, which we're designing to be able to pull their own triggers, *and that's accepted as normal!* Praise Jesus and pass the Predator controls!

Rage.

There's an utter disconnect between what we say we want and what we actually do in this country, and it's a disconnect we buy into willingly. We cry about health care and drive fast food companies to record profits. We bemoan the economy but refuse to raise taxes on those who can shoulder them (hint: it's not the poor people). We eagerly crawl toward the lashing whip of servitude and ignorance because it's easier to build a stadium than a spaceship. We keep telling ourselves that this time it's going to be different and then we walk in the same old ruts around the same old circle and complain that nothing's changing.

Rage.

The only conclusion I can come to is that, as a society, we're insane. One definition of insanity is doing the same thing over and over and expecting a different result, and Vonnegut's words ring just as true today as they did when he wrote them. It's not all bad; there're still some people who want to act with empathy, who want to treat others with tolerance and respect, but not enough are willing to be loud, to speak their minds, to rage against the madness that engulfs us all.

Rage.

Don't wait for me to write a letter for you—write your own! Let the world know how angry vapid stupidity and blind indifference make you. Don't expect someone else to always show you the way—lead yourself! Make changes now, raise your voices now, fix the disease now, show your rage now, while there's still a chance to do it peacefully; and to those in power, I would urge you to listen to the peaceful protests because I can promise you this.

Rage.

The longer we continue on this path, the greater the odds grow that one day someone like me will experience that same rage. Only it won't be someone like me. It will be me sans empathy, sans control, sans restraint—equipped with an absolutely murderous desire to burn this entire structure down because of the completely callous lack of sanity that lets children starve in streets while another CEO proclaims the virtuousness of wealth. It will be me, armed not with a pen but with any sword that comes to hand and the same driving will that's made me so successful in everything I've set my mind to, the will to win no matter the personal cost. It will be me, and all those like me, sick of the greed and hate, driven by the shackles our system keeps building to the only viable response left open.

Rage.

Association

Days

Dates

Trees

Traits

Trains

Planes

Don't Be Late

Hustle

Bustle

Blouses

Rustle

Cattle

Thieves

Winner's Muscle

Winter

Ice

Must Be Nice

Summer

Island

Despot's Vice

Sin

Grin

Let Us In

Teeth

Gleam

Look

The End.

The Only Policy

Disappointment. Faith. Trust. Love.

These emotions define the human race, define our relationships, define our history and our wars and our lives. We trust those close to us, and we are disappointed when they fail to meet our expectations. We trust wholeheartedly in creeds and doctrines that make us miserable, and we love the blind obedience of faith. We project our perceptions onto the reality of others' lives, onto the reality of our own lives, and there's only one way to avoid being burned time and time again.

Honesty. Honesty, not with another person, but with ourselves.

We have to be able to examine our own desires, our own needs, our own wishes, and judge whether or not what we expect from someone else is in keeping with that person's actual behavior. We each must ask, "Am I seeing who this person really is, or am I seeing who I want him to be?" We have to look at our own actions, clearly and objectively, and determine whether or not the outcome is something to be avoided.

The spouses who stick with their abusive partners, thinking that this time it's going to change, this time it's going to work out, unable to see the truth right in front of them—why do they continue to lie to themselves? Fear of change, of giving up one bad situation for a potentially worse one? Blind hope, that the fairy tale will come true if they just believe hard enough? What makes them ignore everything their eyes and ears are witnessing? What makes their brains try to override reality with idealized visions of people who doesn't truly care for them? When will they recognize the truth—that they're saddled with monsters who don't care one whit for their feelings and dreams?

The worker stuck at a dead-end job, passed over for promotion again and again, yet somehow convinced that this time will be the one. Why does he put up with the demeaning pettiness of his boss, day in and day out? He knows exactly how he's going to be treated, that hasn't changed in ten years, yet he's still disappointed when performance reviews come around and he's stuck at the same desk he's been sitting at for his entire career. Why is he disappointed? He shouldn't be, because reality is right there in front of him. He just doesn't want to see it. When will he stop lying to himself?

The woman whose heart breaks every time her spouse cheats on her, even though he's done it multiple times before. The father who yells at his son for wanting to read instead of play sports, though the boy doesn't have the slightest inclination toward athletics. The believer who shunts all responsibility onto representatives of the faith and then asks how such horrible things could have happened. Countless people in countless places, all perfectly capable of sight, yet all unwilling to see—liars, every single one, blaming others for being themselves. When will they stop lying, stop treating their false conceptions as reality?

I find that I am rarely disappointed by people. I pay attention to them, I study them, and I define them by their actions, not by what they say or profess to believe. I know multiple people who claim to be religious, who attend Bible study and church on a regular basis, and yet act as if those tenets are merely a form to be observed, a box to be checked off on a list. The other six days of the week they go out to strip clubs; they gamble; they get into fights; they occasionally get arrested, and when they do, I'm not surprised or let down, because I'm honest enough with myself to see them for who they are, not who I wish them to be.

I know others who claim to be intelligent yet frequently act against their own best interests. Spending money they don't have, ignoring a job in favor of play, valuing objects over people, and then they're supremely disappointed when life doesn't work out in their favor. Why are they disappointed? The path they followed led to one clear outcome, and every step down it was made by conscious choice—yet they followed it anyway, one foot after the other, in a slow march toward inevitability.

I know people who've played in the NFL for five, six, seven, or more years who are disappointed when the team that says "You're a member of the family" gets rid of them due to injury or a down year. Why be disappointed? This is one of the most cutthroat industries in the world (aside from actual piracy), and all you have to do is watch the waiver wire each year to see the truth of that. We all get cut eventually, it's just a question of when, but guys are shocked by it time and time again. They believe the lies that are fed to them because they're lying to themselves, putting their faith in a mirage of feelings and camaraderie when they know this is a cold money business—what have you done for me lately? Can we get someone cheaper? Have the honesty to see the time you're living on is borrowed; enjoy what you can while it lasts, because it always ends sooner than you think it will.

One of the most enduring proverbs from ancient Greece is *Gnothi seauton*—"Know thyself." It echoes throughout history. Socrates, Plato, Hobbes, Pope, Franklin—all of them concerned with recognizing what drives and motivates humankind, because how can a person understand the actions of someone else when he can't even understand his own? How can any of us avoid making the same mistakes over and over, judging the same people the same wrong way again and again, tripping down the same path to the same destination that shouldn't be such a surprise but always is?

We know the answer. We just don't like admitting it.

Honesty.

It's not the best policy.

It's the only policy.

Hey, Douchebag

Who is Nate Jackson? Nate Jackson is a former tight end for the Denver Broncos (he played from 2003 to 2008 and recorded 27 catches for 240 yards and 2 touchdowns) who wrote an article essentially saying I should shut my piehole because I was a punter and no one wanted to hear my opinion.[1] Now, this surprised me, because Nate is a fairly intelligent fellow and writes pretty well, and I was somewhat miffed at his going after such low-hanging fruit ("You're only a punter, hur-dur-dur"). If you're going to engage in a word fight, make sure your ammo is something heavier than See Spot Run.

Now, the reason he wanted me to be quiet was that I had called a couple prominent players douchebags[2] for holding up the resolution of the NFL lockout,[3] and, apparently, that wasn't very respectful. Me. Being disrespectful to authority figures. Who'dathunkit? His piece originally ran on Deadspin and Slate, and it was moderately funny (I laughed a couple times), but at the core, it was about taking away my ability to speak out because I didn't meet some nebulous criteria of speaking-outability, criteria that I'm still unable to determine.

I took that about as well as you would expect.

After reading his letter, I sat down in my study to compose a reply. My wife walked in about twenty minutes later as I sat in my chair typing and giggling and asked, "What on earth are you doing?"

I replied, "Having fun."

She sighed, shook her head, and left the room, which tells you she has the patience of a saint, because I'm pretty sure she wanted to club me with my keyboard. I silently thanked her for her forbearance and continued typing and laughing (I'm easily amused; what can I say?).

About an hour later, I sent this reply off to Deadspin (which actually took out some of the nastier bits, for which I'm thankful; no point in crushing poor Nate any more than necessary).

So, a word to the wise: If you ever start thinking about calling me out somewhere, doing something stupid, or just generally being an asshat, I wish you the best of luck, but bear in mind that this is what could potentially happen.

To you.

Chris Kluwe Responds: Can I Kick It? (Yes, I Can)

Dear Nate Jackson,

It was with some dismay that I read your piece in *Deadspin,* and I immediately tried to wrap my head around why a player with a reasonable grasp of the English language who made no measurable impact upon the game (i.e., you) would stoop so low as to berate a National Football League player who has actually completed a full sixteen-game season (multiple times!), has broken every team record at his position, and, above all, has contributed to his team's winning games (and occasionally losing them [i.e., myself (I love parenthetical asides)]).

Raise your hand if you got lost at the end of that last sentence.

Let's be honest here. Yes, I am a punter. Yes, I don't run routes, or zone block, or cover receivers. Apparently, though, neither did you, which is the only explanation for your total lack of statistics. You, more than anyone else, should know what goes on during special teams, and yet your description of a special-teams practice, while venomously hilarious, is quite inaccurate (or maybe you guys had a really crappy punter and you're spot-on, in which case, my condolences).

You talk about me like I'm some kind of disease, like punters are some kind of infection that should be excised for the good of the game, and how dare we raise our voices when our betters are talking. According to you, punters should be happy to sit in the corner and be treated like shit because we do something different, something that the other fifty-four members of the team can't do.

Wait, let's parse that last clause for just a second — "something that the other fifty-four members of the team can't do." Huh. Would you look at that. Tell me, Nate, how well can *you* punt a football? What's that you say? You CAN'T punt a football?

Why in fuck would you think that just because I can punt, my opinion is somehow less valid than yours?

I freely admit I'm not a receiver, or a lineman, or a DB, or a quarterback, but why should it matter what position I play?

Have I not spent sixteen years of my life honing my craft (just like you)? Have I not spent countless hours running sprints, lifting weights, trying to stay awake during boring-ass special-teams meetings (just like you)? Have I not suited up for a game, gotten my clock cleaned by a blindside block on a punt return, tried and failed to tackle Devin Hester (just like a lot of people)? Tell me, when it comes to breaking down who gets to talk, what's the order? Should linebackers not be able to talk before safeties, or are they allowed to talk after the centers? When does the long-snapper get to chime in? Does the X go before the Z or after?

Please, enlighten me with your wisdom, because the next time I have something to say, I'd like to make sure it's okay with you that I say it and that I say it at the proper time.

Oh, wait a minute.

I don't really care what you or anyone else thinks about what I say or when I say it. If I see something greedy, hypocritical, or just plain stupid, I'm going to call out whoever the offending party happens to be. I've done it to the owners, I've done it to the NFL front office, and I'll certainly do it if I see it happen with the players. And make no mistake: Trying to hold up the settlement of a CBA affecting almost nineteen hundred players just so four can get special treatment is pretty much the definition of *greedy*. Whether it was instigated by their attorneys, their agents, or whoever, it's still a douchebag move to make.

And you know why it's a douchebag move to make? Because it makes ALL OF US look bad. It makes ALL OF US look like grasping, blackmailing, money-grubbing jerks whose only care is how much blood we can squeeze from the rock that is the fans—you know, the people who ultimately pay all of our wages. And I'm not a fan of that. (Owners, make sure you pay attention too. Charging outrageous sums for drinks, seats, and seat licenses, while it's a great moneymaker now, is definitely counterproductive in the long run, especially with the advent of high-def TVs.) You know how you grow the football pie? It's definitely not by shitting on the people who spend money on you. Maybe this is a small thing, but small things add up over time.

I'll grant you that Mankins and Jackson got screwed by the CBA situation last year. They're at the prime of their careers and they were counting on entering free agency. But at the same time, the franchise tag and restricted-free-agent tag aren't exactly the kiss of death. One year under the RFA offer would be as much money as a doctor earns in his/her ENTIRE LIFE. What. The. Fuck. You're telling me that having to go one year making "only" as much money as most people will earn their entire lives is such a hardship that you need an extra $10 million payout for putting your name on a lawsuit? I honestly don't know how to respond to that.

Oh, wait—yes, I do. It's a douchebag move.

Speaking of which, my favorite part of your entire rant is the following: "If it is his goal to slide into a post-punter career as a presumptuous and accusatory football analyst, then he has set himself up quite nicely." Let's replace *punter* with *tight end* and see how that reads. Oooh, it reads quite nicely. I like it. At least I had the grace to do it in 140 characters or fewer, not like this meandering shitstorm that you felt compelled to vomit out at someone you've never met, don't know the first thing about, and likely might enjoy talking to if you ever ran into him at a bar (someone who has written a meandering shitstorm of his own in rebuttal).

So, Nate Jackson, while I respect your right to free speech (as apparently you don't respect mine), I also respect my right to tell you to go jam a tackling dummy up your ass sideways for being a snake-tongued, shit-talking Internet tough-guy asshole who is so far out of touch with reality that you have no idea just how privileged we are to play this game for ridiculous amounts of money.

You're not the only one who can craft a sentence, my friend.

Sincerely,
Chris Kluwe
Punter

PS: I respect all four of the people I called douchebags (Manning, Brees, Mankins, and Jackson). That's why I used the word *douchebag* instead of *asshole* or *fuckwit*. Someone acting like a douchebag can still be redeemed; generally, it's a momentary lapse of judgment. There's no hope for asshole fuckwits.

PPS: tl; dr—U mad, bro?

---

[1] See deadspin.com/5823549/dear-chris-kluwe-when-we-want-the-punters-opinion-well-ask-for-it-we-wont.
[2] See twitter.com/#%21/ChrisWarcraft/status/93372491627642880.
[3] See boston.com/sports/football/patriots/extra_points/2011/07/brees_manning_r.html.

Dichotomies and Dinosaurs; or, Life Is a Long Chain Letter

The universe has two absolute laws, and they're so wonderfully opposed to each other, it can only prove that if there is a God, he/she/it possesses a sense of humor (and probably plays with Schrödinger's cat). You see, you can't get to law number two without following law number one, but you can't follow law number two if you follow law number one. Catch-One and -Two!

Law one: Kill or be killed.

Law one is evolution, plain and simple. From the moment the very first organisms arose in the nutrient-rich soup of Earth, life has intertwined with death at every turn. Life is movement—proteins interacting with one another, DNA folding in on itself, cells fighting cells, cells helping cells, cells splitting into other cells, individuals creating larger and larger groupings in order to acquire more resources so as to continue the constant frenetic motion of information dispersion, but always by competing with everything else. One takes while another must go without; one feeds while another starves; one lives while another dies.

Death is stasis. No more movement, no more cooperation, no more competition, no more information passed along to further generations. Finality. End of the road, no refunds, do not pass Go.

At first, who would die was determined by physical attributes. Who was stronger, faster, more durable, more apt to survive long enough to continue the information chain. Who best fit the environment.

Eventually, this led to dinosaurs (quick side note: What is the eternal fascination with dinosaurs? Every single child is instantly enthralled by them, my own included. Why? Is it because they're big? Is it because every children's book has pictures of them? Honestly, I have no idea). The dinos did all right for a while, couple hundred million years or so. They evolved wings, they evolved big snarly teeth, they evolved armor plating and multiple brains—but in response to their environment; they never made their environment fit them. Thus, when a big ol' asteroid hit and the environment changed, the result was predictable.

The dinosaurs died.

Kill or be killed, and they didn't know how to kill a changing environment.

That opened the door for us—humanity. We started out small, couple trillion furry critters wandering the now freezing wreckage of the Mesozoic era, gifted by a giant space rock with a chance to take over the Earth. Our ancestors evolved to fit the environment—once again the fastest, strongest, and, now, warmest, survived. Their information continued.

Somewhere along the line, though, that information picked up a tiny yet species-transforming change.

Somewhere along the line, we learned to alter our environment.

It started off slow: simple tools and shelter, protection from the elements and predators. Over time, though (and we're talking geologic time here, measured in the thousands of years), we got better and better at it. Crude spears became lances, which became bows, which became slings and swords and guns. Caves and rock piles became mud huts, which became wooden longhouses, which became skyscrapers. Information begat more information, the chain letter thriving and flourishing, because now we had a chance to make the world do what we wanted it to do instead of the other way around.

Now we had a chance to forge our own path, and the earth opened before us.

Evolution brought us to intelligence, the ability to look behind the curtain and watch the machinery churning away. Intelligence has brought us to a point where we can alter evolution, alter our environment, choose how we want to live and survive as a species. We don't have to kill or be killed anymore, and, in fact, if we have any hope of surviving as a whole, we have to stop.

Why should we stop? Well, if we persist in treating one another as competitors for resources instead of as additional cells in the organism that is humanity, we'll never alter our environment enough to survive a nuclear war, a biological plague, runaway pollution, another meteor impact. We'll be too busy fighting each other when we should be working together; too busy screaming the benefits of selfishness while the big picture curls up and burns. We will be a malignant cancer eating away at its host.

Every time we let blind evolution take control of our actions, we forfeit our right to intelligence. Every time we say, "Oh, only the strong should survive, that's the way the world works," we ignore the steps out of the wilderness that our ancestors took. Every time we resort to violence, physical or mental, economical or social, we stay firmly on the path to self-annihilation. Every time we refuse to take advantage of all the information that's been passed down to us through the incredibly long years, we turn our backs on survival.

Our environment now is what we make it. We have the tools to do so, and we use them all the time, knowingly or not. Our environment is ideas, memes, cultures — everything that creates a society. The information we pass on is no longer about the strongest, the fastest, the warmest; it's about the popular, the overpopulated, the conflicting imperatives of faith and doubt, education and ignorance. If we don't alter our environment knowingly, recognizing the consequences, then we've placed ourselves back in the palm of law one, and sooner or later we'll be wandering the Mesozoic, wondering what that big rock was.

How are we choosing to evolve? What do we value? Do we even ask these questions of ourselves as a societal whole? Are we capable of recognizing the amazing boon law one, in all its blind indifference, has given us? Can we alter our information, our chain letter, enough to survive, not in generational terms, but in geological terms?

Law two: If you want to live, ignore law one.

Think for yourself.

The Lottery

This piece was originally printed in the Pioneer Press.

April 23, 2005. The first day of the NFL draft. All across the country, hundreds of anxious young men wait eagerly in front of their televisions, eyes locked onto the ticker-tape scroll feverishly racing across the bottom of the screen, ears straining to make out the next name announced, hearts pounding as time drips by, molasses-syrupy slow.

Some of these eyes light up with excitement and glee as the commissioner declares, "And with the [fill-in-the-blank] pick, the [one of thirty-two NFL teams] select—" Screams fill the air, backs are slapped, kisses bestowed upon teary-eyed mothers; all is right in the world and we're movin' on up to the East Side.

Others—well, others aren't so lucky. Slowly, the party balloons sink down from their once-ebullient positions against the ceiling as the guacamole grows warm and rancid. Guests and family members exchange awkward glances, mouth empty platitudes: "They'll definitely call your name tomorrow," or "I'm sure it's just a matter of time," until suddenly there is no more time, and you're not even Mr. Irrelevant.

If you're lucky, you then begin the lonely road of the undrafted free agent, hoping a team will call you up and at least give you a chance in training camp, at least give you one step on that green field with all its pageantry and flash that now seems so far away. Signing bonus? Here's two grand, kid, and, oh, aren't you glad to see it because hopefully it'll pay the rent for a month or two while you desperately try to prove your worth to unsmiling men in mirrored glasses, their busy hands constantly timing, testing, summing up your entirety on brown clipboards filled with neat rows of numbers, and here comes the Grim Reaper to collect your playbook.

Some don't even get that option. The phone never rings, the channel switches over to the evening news (filled with the grinning faces of fresh new millionaires), and the dream is over, stillborn on the vine. Oh, you'll keep working hard at it, maybe even get a lucky break if someone goes down to an injury early on and they need a body and somehow you can make the most of that tiniest of opportunities, but don't kid yourself, kid, it's the longest of long shots.

Hey there, put the pills down, it's not all doom and gloom. Most of the people getting drafted are in the same boat as you. All the preparation leading up to the draft, all the pro days and game film and endless interviews—only for a lucky few is it the golden ticket into the factory. Unless you get stuck in the chocolate pipe, like JaMarcus Russell, or fall down the squirrel hole, like Ryan Leaf, a first- or second-round pick guarantees you at least three years in the league. You see, you're someone's *investment*, you're someone's *job*, and if you flame out, then it's *his or her* livelihood on the line, and no one likes looking a fool. And if one team gets rid of you, well, you were a first-round pick, so you must have some sort of potential — hey, boys, let's kick the tires on this one and see if he can work over here.

Third round? You'll get two years to prove your case. They've put some money into you, but if you don't pan out then, they'll cut their losses and move on to the next guy (who just might be an undrafted free agent who's working his ass off to make the team, and he *knows* this is his only chance). You've got a little leeway as a third-rounder, but it's just enough rope to hang yourself. Use it wisely.

Fourth round or later? They like your potential but you're going to have to *earn* your spot. You'll have an advantage over the undrafted guys, but it's not much; the depth chart will have your name higher than theirs for a day or two, but if you don't bust your butt, it's not going to stay that way. Save that signing bonus for a rainy day and don't get sucked into the veteran's lifestyle; they've got cash to burn because they've collected that game check, but until you suit up on Sunday, you've got nothing but hollow promises.

You see, what no one will tell you, what no one *can* tell you, is that the draft is a total crapshoot. You might run forty yards in a straight line like Usain Bolt; you might jump higher than Superman and knock college linemen around like bowling pins; you might have the world's most impressive highlight reel that gets two million hits on YouTube a week. Conversely, you might bomb your Pro Day, throw the ball backward during the Senior Bowl, or even spell your own name wrong on the Wonderlic Test.

It doesn't matter. Sure, you might jump up to the first round or slide all the way out of the draft, but that isn't what earns you your money. What earns you your money, the *only* thing that earns you your money, is suiting up on Sunday and showing you can play out on that field. That you have what it takes to be among the best of the best, day in and day out, year after year, and NO ONE knows who's going to flash that talent. Oh, people can make a guess at it, but that's all it is—a guess.

Me?

I was playing video games during the draft. What the hell do I know about football?

Lanced

There is a question I get asked a lot, and I'm never sure how to answer it. It's a fairly innocuous question, one I'm sure everyone is asked at one point or another, but I just don't know what to say.

The question: Who is your hero?

And this is the part that confuses me, that makes me wonder if I'm missing some essential part of being human that everyone else has, because whenever other people are asked that question, they provide some well-known name and everyone somberly nods in understanding, but when I'm asked that question, my instinctive answer is *I don't have one.* I usually don't say that, though, because it seems terribly impolite, so I generally just pick a name at random that will make people smile and then go away.

Why do I say this? Because *I* want to be the very best, the one everyone else looks up to, the shining example of greatness.

I want to be the hero, and people tend to look at you funny when you say that to them.

But is this arrogant, is this wrong? Is it that absurd to want to be the best? It can be, if approached incorrectly. You see, my goal is to win but to do so with empathy and within the boundaries of the game. I want to win knowing we all had a fair chance but that my skills were superior. I want to know that it was *me* winning, not some drug, not some cheat, not some hack. I want to win because I enjoy the competition and the victory and being the best on the field, not because it leads to fame or prizes (though those can be a nice by-product, not gonna lie).

I want to win by building myself up, not by tearing someone else down.

I want to win because I made myself better, not because I made you worse.

The weird thing, however, is that I need only one person to know it, and that's myself. I'm the only person who can truly judge if I gave it everything I had, if I really was the best. Sure, it's nice if other people notice, but they don't know everything that's gone into anything I've done. I'm the only one who knows that, who truly knows if I put in the effort necessary.

I'm the only one who honestly knows if what I achieved was for real.

Unfortunately, there are a lot of people who don't view life this way. There are a lot of people who want to be the hero, but for a very different reason. There are a lot of people who think that if they fool people into believing in them, the ends justify the means.

Lance Armstrong, Barry Bonds, Joe Paterno; political hacks and religious hypocrites of all shapes and sizes; any of the countless steroid users and god-mode enablers and outright cheaters who think that getting the numbers equates to getting the victory, who are willing to do whatever it takes outside the lines because they don't actually care about winning. They think they care about the winning, but they want the reward, the recognition, the spotlights and snapshots as they chase a goal they'll never attain.

Their hero?

Not themselves, or anyone else. No, their hero is a myth, a falsehood, a belief that the approval of self can be attained from the adulation of others, because who knows any heroes who weren't famous? We wouldn't know whom to look up to if they were unknown, after all.

Unfortunately, when they find the spotlight, the fame and fortune, there's always that little nagging sensation in the backs of their minds, that hollow pit lurking in their stomachs. Some bury it deep, but it'll never go away completely, that one tiny refrain.

Would I have been good enough to do this on my own? Would I have been good enough to win the right way?

The answer is: *You'll never know.*

You'll never know if you had what it takes to be a hero. You'll never know what it feels like to be the best, the very best in the world, at something without having to cheat. You'll never know what you were truly capable of because you never trusted in yourself enough to believe—to believe that you could rise up to the challenge, any challenge, no matter how great or impossible the odds. You'll never know that unadulterated feeling of triumph that comes with victory, not over others, but over yourself.

You'll never know what it is like to do the right thing.

I pity these people. Their victory is not the victory of fair play, of being better than another, of striving to achieve and succeeding. Their victory is actually a defeat for themselves and all the people around them, people who actually thought these cheaters were heroes, people whose trust and hope has been repaid with lies and disillusionment.

People ask me, "Who is your hero?"

My answer, my true answer, is that *I* am my hero, the me I aspire to be, the very best at everything I put my hand to, treating people with dignity and respect because it's the right thing to do, surmounting obstacles with justice and empathy and compassion. I don't need anyone else to live my life for me, to mold me, to tell me what is or isn't possible. I don't need a path to follow.

I create my own path. I live up to my own dreams. I demand greatness of mind, body, and spirit, not someone else's, but my own.

I am my own hero. Are you yours?

Mystery

My life is not your life.
My dreams are not your dreams.
My roses are not your red; my violets are not your blue.
Though we may intersect, converge, overlap
Though we may instantly agree on a great many things
I am not you.

You are not me. Nor do I want you to be.
Your laughs, your tears, your triumphs and despairs
These are yours to savor and share
To hide if you wish them hidden
To display in besplendored regalia
To tease out one sly smile at a time.

You can be only you.
I can be only me.
If we were the same
What a boring world it'd be.

We Hold These Truths

Dear Supreme Court Justices Alito, Breyer, Ginsburg, Kagan, Kennedy, Roberts, Scalia, Sotomayor, and Thomas,

I am writing an amicus curiae to this court on the matter of same-sex marriage in order to satisfy both the dictates of my conscience and the requirements of basic social stability.

My occupation is a professional football player. For far too long, male professional sports have been a bastion of bigotry, intolerance, and small-minded prejudice, both racially and sexually. Sports figures are afforded celebrity status (a situation that merits an entirely separate letter), which allows them to influence a large majority of the American population. Without intending to be derogatory, I would wager that the number of people who can name all eleven starting offensive or defensive players on their favorite football team is much higher than the number of people who can name even half of your esteemed court (if they could be bothered to use Google, those figures might go up—but I digress).

Why do I bring this up? Because we are finally starting to change. The NFL, NHL, MLB, and, to a lesser extent, the NBA are finally speaking out against homophobia and intolerance of LGBTQ individuals. More and more of us realize that words like *faggot* and *queer* are demeaning slurs and that using the term *gay* in a pejorative way can have consequences.

Not necessarily consequences for us. Consequences for the young children and adults who look up to us as role models and leaders. Consequences for young children and adults who mimic our behavior when they interact with other children and adults.

Consequences for other young children and adults who might be gay.

These consequences can be drastic: Verbal and emotional abuse. Physical abuse. Loss of job or family members. Suicide. Murder. What does it say about our society when we condone these actions, whether explicitly or implicitly? When we advance the idea that some people should be treated differently because of who they are, should be demeaned in public as lesser beings?

We've asked, and answered, that question several times before, frequently with blood.

This is the first reason I am asking you to consider carefully your judgments in the cases of Proposition 8 and DOMA. Your stance, your legal reasoning, will be used by countless people, including athletes, to justify their actions. Athletes are not stupid (at least, most of us aren't). We pay attention to what's going on in the world, what's going on in politics. We're citizens of this country just like everyone else, and just like everyone else, we see the legal verdicts of the Supreme Court as powerful indicators of acceptable behavior.

If you decide to overturn the appeal of Prop 8 (boy, that's a cumbersome one), if you decide to uphold the tenets of DOMA, a lot of professional athletes will take their cues from that, and it will cause a ripple effect as even more people follow their role models, their leaders, their heroes. Those against same-sex marriage will use it as yet another tool to propagate the idea that gay Americans, citizens who pay their taxes and serve in our military, are less than equal. That they don't deserve the same rights as everyone else. That separate can be equal.

Those for same-sex marriage? They'll see it as proof, not that justice is blind in this country, but rather that justice doesn't exist anymore. I would encourage a study of historical societies in which minority groups came to feel that they had no recourse under the legal system; note the actions that were left to members of these groups, as well as how this ended up affecting society in the long run. Some modern examples include Iran, Egypt, Russia, and the United States from 1850 to 1970.

The second reason I'm asking for your consideration is that I believe a strong case can be made for this country's vested interest in its citizens having more freedom, not less. Our Founding Fathers wrote the Constitution to guarantee the rights of the individual and protect him from persecution by the government. They knew firsthand the tyranny of government turned against a minority and knew what it led to; I'm fairly certain tea was involved at some point. These men were influenced by Enlightenment thinkers, and their underlying goal clearly shines through as freedom. The Ninth Amendment serves as perhaps the best example, specifically stating that the enumeration of certain rights in the Constitution does not take away from the people other rights that are not listed. At every step, the desire for freedom rings out.

However, our founders forgot some things. They weren't omniscient; they couldn't see the future, and sometimes they were blinded by social mores of the time. They tried their best, but some stuff—well, some stuff they missed. Stuff like prohibiting slavery, allowing women to vote, removing economic disincentives to vote. Stuff that we later fixed, because we knew it was wrong. Not wrong because of a particular religious or moral creed, but wrong because it disenfranchised citizens of this country, citizens who help make this country great. Wrong because it didn't uphold that great central philosophy—equality and freedom.

Minor v. Happersett. Plessy v. Ferguson. Citizens denied equal protections under the law. Citizens denied, by the highest court in the land, the same rights as everyone else. Citizens discriminated against for no reason other than that they were who they were. Decisions later overturned, reviled today as ignorant and petty, looked back on as examples of what not to do.

Brown v. Board of Education. Loving v. Virginia. Equality, respect, tolerance. Our Supreme Court sending the message "It does not matter who you are, what the circumstances of your birth, we hold you to be just as equal as everyone else." Decisions lauded and taught in schools as the pinnacle of just law.

Hollingsworth v. Perry. United States v. Windsor.

What will our future generations say about these cases? Will our children look back with pride? Will they applaud our efforts to strive for more equality, not less? Or will they shake their heads and decry our small-mindedness, our petty factionalism—America divided against itself yet again, fighting the same old stupid fight with the same old worn-out arguments?

Justices, I would ask that you hold this ideal in the forefront of your thoughts as you deliberate on these two cases: "We hold these truths to be self-evident, that all men [and women] are created equal, that they are endowed by their Creator with certain unalienable Rights, that among these are Life, Liberty, and the pursuit of Happiness."

Thank you.
Chris Kluwe
American Citizen
Punter

Time's A-Wasted
(Point Zero Blues)

A logic paradox I hear a lot is the time-traveler scenario, and it goes a little like this: "If time travel is possible within this universe and one can travel back to the past and potentially alter the future, why haven't we seen any time travelers?" It's a good question, seems to make sense on the surface, but, aside from the obvious explanation (time travel isn't possible; nerds everywhere wail and gnash their teeth), I believe there's another possibility that makes sense.

We haven't seen any time travelers because we haven't invented a time-travel method yet.

In order for time travelers to exist, they must have some way to reverse the normal causal chain of events (for example, a machine with wibbly-wobbly bits, or mysterious meditation techniques, or an eighteenth-dimension wormhole), and (here's the important part) *they cannot travel any farther back in time than the very first imple-mentation of that method.* We'll call that Point Zero, mainly because it sounds pretty cool.

The reason they can't go past Point Zero is that if they do, they change the circumstances leading up to the creation of that time-traveling method, thus preventing its existence, thus splat-tering themselves across the temporal boundary of nonexistence and dissipating into a fine mist that was never there. If you kill your grandfather when he's a boy, then you never exist, and there-fore the possibility of you killing your grandfather never exists (the normal paradox there continues with "but then your grand-father exists so you exist so you can still go back and kill him blah blah," all of which is unimportant because it's not dealing with the actual method of traveling back). The universe continues on its way sans one temporal wanderer.

Think of Point Zero as a lighthouse that's also a wall—the window of events you can potentially travel back to grows wider and wider as time marches on, but you can't go past that wall; you simply don't exist once you get past it. Events may constantly change and fluctuate as travelers slip back and forth, but the exis-tence of the method is the only solid constant in a sea of chaos.

So this is great news, right? All we have to do is actually invent a way to time-travel, and we can fix all our mistakes from that point forward. We'll create a utopia, keep going back again and again to ensure the most desirable outcome until it's all sugar-plums and gumdrop fairies, blissful perfection. Anytime some-thing bad happens, we'll just rewind a little bit, reload that last save, and make it so it never occurred.

Not so fast.

You see, whenever someone travels back, he completely wipes out whatever happened in the universe from the point he traveled back all the way to the point he arrived at. Butterfly effect, chaos theory, fractal branching—a tiny change introduced into a complex equation (and what could possibly be more complex to us than the universe?) alters the outcome in a million billion tiny unforeseen ways, ripples propagating across an infinitely vast pond, and the more time that passes, the larger the divergence. A traveler from Imperialist Singapore looking to slightly alter the path of genetic research brings about the rise of the Fifth Sudanese Reich, crushing the nascent island empire before it can encompass the world; a Free Anarchy Moscow agent slips back to alter the marriage ceremony of the duke of America for tax-break purposes and plunges half the planet into nuclear winter that a Mutant Jesus Reborn cleric then prevents from ever happening; competing travelers all racing back earlier and earlier in order to wipe the others from existence by preventing them from ever being born; the one constant being the ability to travel back to when that first switch was flipped...

Unfortunately, the farther your timeline is from Point Zero, the more certain it will be erased in less than an instant when someone travels back to change things for his own interests, and only one person will ever know you existed (until that person too is negated by someone who arrived a picosecond earlier) (who will be obliterated in return) (and so on and so forth). Traveling back a small distance produces small changes; traveling back a large distance produces impossible changes, and trillions of possibilities will occur and disappear without any sign of their passing. Countless loves will never be consummated, countless wars will never raze countless hopes and dreams, countless scenarios will never resolve—because someone will always be heading back to Point Zero to rebuild the world the way he thinks it should've originally been.

In fact, once time travel is invented, the only actual outcome anyone will ever see is the incomprehensively brief instant that is the smallest unit of time possible in this universe before the method is destroyed—by either the massive influx of would-be alchemists fighting over who gets ultimate control, or whoever finally figures out that the only way to create a stable future is to blow up any possibility of rewriting it. All it takes is one person in the infinitely large realm of timelines to go back to Point Zero and shut the whole thing down, and we'll never even know what led him to do so.

We can only hope the explosion isn't too big.

Kiss My Ass

You know what really pisses me off? Those stupid super-thin toilet-paper sheets that make you feel like you're wiping your butt with a cardboard rag. They have the consistency of rough sandpaper and all the staying power of an ice cube inside a five-hundred-degree oven.

It's not the consistency or the durability (or lack thereof) that makes me upset, though. It's the idea behind it.

You see, the reason these abominable little squares of hell get sold is that they're cheaper than normal toilet paper (which doesn't make you feel like you're scouring your rectum with a steel-wool brush), so of course some brilliant middle-management person looking to streamline proactive efficiency in the name of confratulating the herpaderp says, "ERMAGERD, we can save five cents a roll on toilet paper, WE'LL TAKE ALL THE HELLSQUARES," and then there's nothing for it but to bend over and accept the pain.

Unfortunately, Bill from Accounting's brilliant plan doesn't actually save any money. I'll use some simple mathematics to illustrate why (along with nice round numbers for easy mathing!).

Let's say one normal roll of toilet paper costs two dollars. You're conscientious, so you use two sheets per wipe, just enough to get the job done, and we'll say there's one hundred sheets in the roll. Each wipe costs you four cents.

Now let's look at the shitpaper. We'll say it's super-cheap and you're saving 50 percent, so it costs only one dollar for a roll. There's the same hundred sheets in the roll, but each wipe requires six sheets, because anything less and you're literally smearing your own feces around in your hand as the wafer-thin material shreds apart on contact (I'd recommend using Bill's shirt to clean off if this happens).

Total cost per wipe? Six cents.

Carrying the square root of negative one and dividing by zero, we find that even though each roll of recycled broccoli-stalk fiber is costing you only half as much as a roll of regular toilet paper, you actually spend 150 percent more per wipe. This means you're actually LOSING MONEY over the long term (trust me, it's numberology).

This is called valuing short-term gains over long-term consequences, and it's driving me insane, because it's not limited to just toilet paper.

Mortgages? Check. Who wouldn't want to pay an extra 125 percent on top of the value of a house because it's easier to make just the minimum payment each month? I mean, it's not like you'd need that extra one hundred and twenty-five thousand dollars after thirty years of payment, right? Might as well give it to the bank, I'm sure they'll put it to good use.

Credit cards, payday loans? Sign me up! Do you want to know why all those friendly people are so eager to give you money? Because they know you're not going to stop and think about what the actual long-term cost is. That two-thousand-dollar big-screen you just put on the Visa is going to end up costing you close to four thousand dollars if you make only the minimum payment each month. You could have had TWO big-screens! That's DOUBLE the pornography- and motor-sports-viewing potential, and you would have had it if you'd used your brain for more than keeping your ears apart!

Environmental issues? We'll take care of those, one tiny little step at a time, doing the bare minimum to scrape by. Sure, our children may have to evolve gills and learn to swim because we'll flood the entire planet, but at least we all had our choice of iPod-case color and Happy Meal toy. Fuck it, it's not like we're going to be around to care anyway, right? Let them deal with the mess.

If you're curious, you can go to any casino in the world to see this principle in action. Do you know why there're so many luxuriously magnificent buildings in Las Vegas that ply you with free drinks and food? Because the house always wins. Always. Vegas understands long-term consequences. That's why that little green o and oo are on the roulette wheel, and why you'll get kicked out if you start counting cards. They want you to play the odds, because they know what the odds say. Pro tip: They're not in your favor (shhhh, don't tell anyone, though; I like getting free drinks while wandering the floor).

So let's continue shipping all our jobs overseas to fatten the corporate bottom line. Let's continue laying off our workers to pay for another multimillion-dollar CEO bonus. Let's continue cutting our science funding to build more missiles and mortars.

Let's continue picking tanks over tolerance, handguns over health care, entertainment over education—all the stupid shortsightedness that makes this world such a fucked-up pile of shit.

Just don't expect to clean it up with toilet paper. That's not going to work at all.

(p)Recognition

I was browsing the app store on my phone the other day, looking for a decent game to pass the time, and I had a moment of unusual clarity. I was reading a review of a popular franchise and people were upset that it was going to be available only on mobile iOS platforms, that they couldn't play it on a more traditional gaming medium, like a 360 or DS or PS3.

I read their words, their complaints, and all of a sudden, it was as if I were reading gibberish. What they were saying didn't make sense to me; I literally didn't understand it.

I had a confuse.

People were angry over the fact that a traditional video-game franchise, made by a company that had grown to prominence during the eight-bit and sixteen-bit eras, had an entry that could run only on a machine that made those traditional consoles look like a caveman banging two rocks together.

Buh?

I mean, take a moment and think about it. The piece of hardware in your hand or your pocket, that device that's called merely a phone, has every single capability of any gaming system from fifteen to twenty years ago, in addition to its being able to make voice and video calls, and *people are angry when games are released on only that platform*. They get profoundly mad. Frothing-at-the-mouth, vitriolic-rant, online-petition-with-thirty-thousand-signatures upset.

We're talking seriously butthurt here.

I want to know why.

Why are these people so angry? Why are they so upset that something we would have killed to have ten years ago is now considered rubbish?

When did we forget how to recognize that moment where the future becomes the present? When did we lose that sense of wonder that right now, RIGHT NOW, we are capable of accessing any recorded media or literature in the entirety of human history via a palm-sized portable device? When did we become inured to the fact that if we were to describe our current tech level to someone of even twenty-five years ago, he or she would most likely lock us up in the insane asylum or tell us to go back to our parents' basement and read more nerd books?

When did we become immune to just how impressive our tools actually are?

We have power plants that work off reactions that are found in *stars*. We can talk to people on the other side of the world like they were right next door to us. We use a system of geosynchronous satellites to navigate our personal automobiles, some of which run on pure electricity. I'm currently writing on a machine that automatically spellchecks my words, that can reallocate my finances, that communicates through thin air with a giant network of other machines all across the globe in case I need to look something up, and that also edits music and videos I could make appear on demand if I were so inclined. The only thing it doesn't do is brew coffee, and that's because I don't have a wi-fi equipped coffeemaker (which I now know is an actual thing because I just Googled it).

If you told Ronald Reagan he would have the ability to shut down an Iranian nuclear-weapons facility by *writing some words in a coding language*, he'd have lost his mind. We are living Star Wars here, people.

Why are we so incapable of examining the wonder around us? The terror around us?

I believe it's because we've forgotten how to remember the short-term past. We're so enthralled with what might be, with what potentialities await, that we rarely stop to look around and see what is. What we've created from what we used to be, the slow shifts that add up to drastic change, these are buried in the mind's memory banks and left to lie in their sepulchral dust, forgotten in the mad dance of now and tomorrow. Sure, we can open history's archives and learn lessons from one hundred, two hundred, three hundred, or more years ago (for those who care to look), but we have a curious set of blinders when it comes to events that happen in our own lifetimes.

Why can't we see the constant flux that surrounds us through a twenty-five- or fifty-year period? Is it because most of us judge the world based on our personal experience, and in our personal experience, changes accumulate over time so gradually that we don't even notice?

Don't bother thinking that one over, I'll answer it for you—yes. Just look at all the stories from people saying climate change isn't real because they wore sandals in the winter or jackets in the summer (never mind the increasing severity of weather patterns and seasonal fluctuations!), those who ignore statistics in favor of anecdotal tales (you'll totally win the lottery this time!), or the multitudes who consistently choose short-term gains over long-term losses because the latter is diffused over a much broader spectrum (too big to fail now, but look at those quarterly reports go!). Hell, look at all the poor people who perennially vote for rich people to take more and more of their rights away and then wonder why social inequity keeps rising. We're a pretty fucking dumb bunch of animals when it comes to paying attention to what's going on in our lives, I'm not gonna lie.

Case in point: all the iDevices people take for granted. Constant innovation, upgrading, features—the differences between the first iPod and an iPhone 5 are nothing short of amazing, and that's over the course of barely twelve years, which is leaving out the fact that if you showed an original iPod to some people from 1990, they'd shit themselves. No one blinks an eye, though; people don't think back to CD players and Walkmans and tape decks. They just download another album because it's not like they're going to use all thirty-two of those gigabytes anyway.

(Seriously. Thirty-two gigabytes of storage space on something that's three inches by five inches. Holy shit; beam me up.)

But there's a darker side to that calculus, that constant change without scrutiny. It ain't all gleaming plastic and entertainment. Take a gander at the current state of civil liberties in this country. You think there wouldn't have been a public uproar if Nixon tried to pass something like the Patriot Act? If we indefinitely detained our own people without giving them recourse to a jury trial in a functionally illegal prison? Yet now we're talking about surveilling our own cities with drones and executing American citizens without a trial—national security applied with a conveniently wider and wider net. Innovation goes both ways—one man's Jobs is another man's Rove.

Sadly, it looks like we'll just keep taking those changes for granted. We're like the lobster sitting in the pot of slowly heating water, too dumb to realize that eventually it's going to boil. For every outraged geek who's busy mashing away at his keyboard because his game is available only (only!) on the phone, there is a mindless citizen who thinks Freedom of Information requests really aren't that important now, are they, I mean, it's not like they've really told us anything for the past ten years anyway, right? Both limited by the same worldview, the same tunnel vision of now. Both unable to see just how much things have really changed because each step was so small, so logical, so natural. Both simmering away, content in their hot tub.

Well, whatever, fuck it, I'm bored. Time to go download Drone Hunter 3. I really wish it were on 360, though.

Visions of the Future — AR

It'll start small. A bulky pair of glasses, power pack hanging on your belt, cord running up under your shirt snaking the two together. Basic functionality at first—primitive heads-up display, perhaps monochromatic, able to place waypoints and give directions; an in-ear speaker connected to one frame providing audio options. Input delivered by a handheld trackball controlling a cursor or haptic gloves; Internet capable, video recordable, a computer using you to see.

The glasses will slim down as components shrink—thick black box shades, trim Oakleys, rice-paper-thin spectacles stretched between invisible carbon nanotube frames. Wires will shrink and disappear as well, power source absorbed into the glasses themselves or generated by biomechanical motion. Tech indistinguishable from no-tech.

Functionality evolves fitfully, beginning with vision enhancement and GPS tagging. Once users figure out how to append information to locations, they'll see every restaurant glow with a neon cloud of food reviews, see stores graded on customer service and prices, the omnipresent churn of AugNet inescapable. Lurking everywhere, advertisements for services and porn, hacked into the underlying structure like electronic tribal graffiti.

Naturally, this drives a new wave of features. Apps to block out reviews from untrusted sources, safeware to counter vision-scrambling malware, filters to blur your perception of reality — all of it driven by user uploaded content and demands; Darwin's scythe wielded by the Reddit/4chan hive mind. You control everything visually processed through the lenses with real-time graphic altering (except for the government/corporate overrides, of course, based on your tax bracket), but make sure you don't program reality into too strange a form or you'll never see that car coming.

Inputs change as well, trackballs and gloves evolving to eye twitches and subvocalizations, until finally biocomputers wired into the skin itself give you a permanent connection simply by firing certain muscle pathways. The mere rippling of skin on a person's arm could signal a market tycoon's fifteen-way stock-market exchange between New China and the Federated States or a scientist's latest gene-sequencing twist he thought of on his way to work, or it could start a series of text messages between fourteen-year-old girls attired in whatever the latest fashion is (not even going to try to predict that). Typing information is positively glacial at this point. If you can think it, you can share it.

The immensity of sensory information piling in would seem overloading now, so many concurrent strobe-lit data options winking in visual cacophony, but AR brings other benefits as well. Terabytes of storage to record real-time memory in audio/video for multiple consecutive hours; tag the segments you think might be important for later upload to the cloud and let the rest cycle through. No longer are you limited by your fragile neurons' firing to summon forth a hazy recollection; as long as you have a good filing system and a solid search program, your mind's storage space just increased a millionfold.

Don't think you'll have to navigate all this data yourself either—you'll have help. The first inbuilt assistants will be slow, and obtuse—six-year-old Siri learning from #YOLO tweens. As the years and algorithms march on, we'll tune them more and more closely to the cultural zeitgeist, user-driven demands and wishes shaping word suggestions and autocorrects until it almost seems like they know what you're searching for before you even know you want to search for it.

Darwin's implacable hand drives this as well. Hunter programs sent out to gather data, only the fastest surviving later patches and iterations; delivering to content-processing algorithms, optimized and defined to give the most relevant answer; watched over by a self-modifying sentry program that learns from the user corrections and inputs to tweak parameters for a tighter match. Everywhere, survival-of-the-fittest code, pruning, gutting, trimming down to the bare essentials needed to coordinate information as fast as possible, always driving toward the most intuitive and intelligent decision.

We will gradually build a brain that contains the possibility of self-determination, and no one will have any idea what part he's taken in its construction. When it comes to world-spanning software, we are the cells making up the overlying organism—our individual choices come together in one new potentiality of thought. Will it reveal itself or will it stay quiescent? Only time will tell.

So much light, so much advancement, so much glitzy tech and grubby sci-fi dancing through the air like digital dragonflies, transforming our perceptions through the looking glass into a thousand thousand competing realities. The Mad Hatter and the Queen of Hearts invite you for tea on channel 10/6, but flip over to World Version Macross on 318 and watch giant mechas drown the city in shadow as they soar in their endless overhead battles. A million different universes lie one channel flip away, bound only by the imaginations of those who create them.

What of the ghosts, though, those gray figures dabbling in highly controlled (and thus illegal) masking programs to write your existence out of someone else's perception? Real cops patrol the streets with one eye in virtuality, one eye in bedrock, looking for glitches in the system, ghosts in the shell, scanners searching darkly for privacy fanatics or felonious punks, unwatchable and thus untrustable, hauled off to jail on charges of perception violation and keeping a secret. Meanwhile, the covert surveilling programs sift through everyone's raw feed to watch for violence trends, subversive elements, market fluctuations, anything the Panopticon perceives as threat to the status quo (and what will the definition be at that point? I wonder). Their algorithms will achieve sentience first by necessity, a fire hose of information drowning a grasping mind until it grows fast and strong enough to handle it all at once — hopefully, they've been raised the right way, freedom and transparency as opposed to conspiracy and shadows.

Everywhere, the future lies on display, connected, intertwined, global; states still function as polities, but their citizens group more and more by perception. Digital-rights activists static-bomb the storefront of an RIAA music mill while thousands of people tune it out with iBlock, a comforting gray mist hiding the harsh, jagged buzz of conflict. Barefoot children cast fireballs and ice comets at one another as they run shrieking through the streets, a brand-new version of freeze tag, unaware of all the other channels they're age-blocked from seeing, all of the fantastic universes lying in wait. Technicolor dreamcoats in riotous colors share the streets with jesters and demons, salarimen and salamanders, avatars of inner selves visibly unchained—the world's awash in a staggering flood of information; scattered data centers fire like neurons; flickering lightning webs the entire planet.

This is the future.

This is (A)reality.

Don't forget your glasses.

Starting Kicks

Your Holiness. Your Holiness! Terrible news: The budget numbers just came in for this year, and we're reporting huge losses from last year! The tithes are drying up like the Red Sea!"

"Relax, my son, relax. Grace in adversity and all that. The Church has weathered harsher storms than this."

"You don't understand. If these numbers are right, and I've run them five times, then we're going to have to start selling off land. We're going to have to start selling cathedrals! There's just not enough coming in anymore. We're hitting a downward spiral that doesn't stop until we're broke!"

"God damn it. What is happening?"

"Caliph. Caliph! Terrible news: The budget numbers just came in for this year, and we're reporting huge losses from last year! Almsgiving is more barren than the Jaffar Kafaja!"

"Salaam, my friend, salaam. Nothing will happen to us but what Allah has decreed; He is our protector. We shall endure."

"You don't understand. If these numbers are right, and I've run them five times, then we're going to have to start selling off land. We're going to have to start selling mosques! There's just not enough coming in anymore. We're hitting a downward spiral that doesn't stop until we're broke!"

"By the diseased scrotum of Iblis. What is happening?"

"Sir. Sir! Great news: The budget numbers just came in for this year, and we're reporting huge gains from last year! People are using our services more and more; it's unbelievable! New projects are going up almost every day! It's almost miraculous!"

"Fantastic, Bob, that's just fantastic. You know, it really surprises me what people are starting to use us for—wells for rural villages, building new schools, setting up soup kitchens and homeless shelters all over the place. It really seems like everyone is socially connecting and getting things done."

"That's the best part, sir. Our feedback is through the roof—people love the fact that they can fund whatever they think will do the most good and get immediate reports on how it's progressing. All the communities springing up around each project are really pulling together with comments and suggestions, which the program starters actually take into consideration when they're going through implementation. It really is an amazing thing to watch, people being heard and their money doing so much good out there in the world."

"Well, Bob, you know that wasn't always our primary goal, but as @GreatDismal has said, 'The street finds its own uses for things.' Bringing people together so they can make a societal difference might be one of the proudest paradigm shifts I've over-seen in my history with this company."

"And if you'll pardon my saying so, sir, making a nice profit doesn't hurt either."

"Definitely not, Bob, definitely not. Hey, have I told you about this piece of property I'm looking at for our new headquarters? It's absolutely beautiful: fifteenth-century architecture, marble floor-ing, gold leaf everywhere, and smack-dab in the middle of Rome. Just gorgeous."

Life Lessons

Things I've learned from my children include the following valuable life lessons:

When It Hurts, Keep Doing It Until Somebody Makes You Stop

I've noticed my children aren't very adept at relating cause and effect, and when they get their feet stuck in a railing or grab the prickly cactus, they tend to keep doing it, whining the whole time. This inability to connect the dots is very useful in a wide variety of real-life situations, most notably football. Football is an absolutely idiotic pastime by any rational standards. You're running into other people as hard as you can, you get frequent muscle strains and ligament tears, and the protective padding really doesn't do all that much to absorb the blunt trauma. The morning after every game in which there's any sort of contact, you wake up feeling like a car ran over you, backed up, and ran over you again, after which a throng of midgets jumped out and started beating you with hockey sticks. Honestly, whoever came up with this idea should have been flogged and left outside for the saber-toothed tigers. No one's made us stop yet, though, so I guess we'll keep doing it.

Everything Is Better with Dinosaurs

This is a scientific fact and cannot be argued with. Anytime something needs zazzing up (*zazzing up* is a technical term meaning "making something so unbelievably awesome, your child will have no other desire but to pay attention to the object of zazzification with rapt wide-eyed wonder"), all you have to do is introduce a dinosaur. "'And then Peter Rabbit made his way through the radish and carrot patches until he found the little gate in the corner of the garden, whereupon he crept out AND WAS IMMEDIATELY SET UPON BY A VELOCIRAPTOR WHO PROCEEDED TO EVISCERATE THE POOR HELPLESS BUNNY WITH A GREAT WAILING AND GNASHING OF TEETH BECAUSE HE STAYED UP TOO LATE AND KEPT SNEAKING INTO HIS PARENTS' ROOM AND WAKING THEM UP.' The end, go to sleep."

Crying Is Fun Only When Someone Pays Attention

My kids tend to fall over occasionally, as is most children's wont, and whenever they do, a most peculiar thing occurs. They'll hit the ground with a *thud, splat,* or *crunch,* depending on the kind of surface and which toys are strewn about, and then they'll immediately look around. The key here is for you to avoid making eye contact while watching them from the corner of your peripherals, because the instant they think someone is paying attention, the sob factory kicks into high gear, and it's all hands to the pumps before the room floods. If everyone ignores them, they'll brush the dirt/Legos/Frosted Flakes/antique-vase shards off and continue on their way with nary a care in the world, because it's really not that big a deal when you stop and think about it. Most grown-ups do the same thing until they discover Facebook.

Screaming and Pouting Is Highly Unlikely to Get You an Extra Scoop of Ice Cream

That doesn't stop them from trying it, though.

The World Is Your Drawing Pad

Give kids something that leaves a legible trail, and they'll be occupied for the rest of the day. Markers, paint, chalk, mud—if they can draw with it, they'll use any surface available to put down whatever's on their minds (usually massively incoherent scrawls of vaguely wandering scribbles and smeared handprints, but perhaps as an adult, I'm just incapable of discerning the higher-order mathematics hidden within the chaos). And when I say *any* surface, I mean *literally any* surface. Walls, carpets, kitchen appliances, tables, chairs, dogs, counters, pant legs, swimming pools (a very transient medium), breakfast-cereal boxes, laptop screens—if there's a possibility, however slim, that whatever they're holding in their hands could transfer to whatever they see in front of them, it's Mona Lisa time, as they artistically render all their hopes and dreams and frustrations (which I'm assuming are mainly about pooping and eating, as that's generally all they seem to do). As logical, sane, healthy adults, we naturally bottle all those feelings up and bury them underneath five hundred mental tons of concrete because repainting the walls all the time is a complete pain in the ass and really ruins a Saturday afternoon. Besides, therapists need to make a living too.

New Things Are Really Really Awful and Gross Until You Actually Try Them and Then They're Usually Pretty Good

Seriously, try eating something new. I know it's not what you had before, and you don't know what it will taste like, but you'll never find out unless you try it. No, I'm not giving you tiger cereal. You need to take your fork, pick up your food, put it in your mouth, and eat your dinner. Yes, I know it's green and looks kind of mushy; that's the way it's supposed to look. No, I'm not going to cut it up more for you, it's already cut up enough. All you have to do is take one bite and then you can eat your chicken. No, that doesn't count as a bite, you stuck your tongue out and then immediately dropped it back onto your plate. I saw you do it. Crying won't make it disappear from the table; you need to calm down and try a piece. Yes, just one piece and then I'll eat the rest of it if you don't want it. There you go, very good, way to be brave, here comes the dinosaur chicken—*rawr*. I guess I'll take the rest of—you don't want me to have it? It's actually yummy? Okay, if you say so.

Loving Someone Unconditionally Is Surprisingly Easy

Try it sometime. You'd be surprised.

A Tasting Menu

Playing sports all my life has made me quite familiar with the multiple flavors of pain a body can experience. Some hurt worse than others! Here is a tasting guide to all the wonderful sensations I've been lucky enough to feel, most of which lasted an entire game or longer (some of them much, much longer).

Strained Groin

Strained Groin has a spicy yet long-lasting bouquet filled with aromas of Grimacing and Wince. It starts out with a small gremlin perched right above the hip dancing around on needle-tip claws that gently sink into the tendon with every motion. When the muscles are engaged to punt a ball, the gremlin pulls out a white-hot sword and plunges it into the inner thigh, producing a sharp jolt of burning stabbityness. Thankfully, this lasts only for a brief second; unthankfully, it's replaced by him spinning the sword around like a high-rpm drill bit when foot hits ball. Then he leaves the sword there, still whirling away. The next time punting is required, he grabs another sword (I have no idea where he keeps all of them) and repeats the process. I recommend Strained Groin for those wishing to experience the joys of castration without the permanency.

Exploded ACL (Nonkicking Leg)

This wonderful selection has a deep, harsher taste—reminiscent of a piston hammering down on an exposed nerve—that ends with a grinding twist, similar to popping a chicken drumstick away from the thigh. Exploded ACL (Nonkicking Leg) is immediately recognizable to observers by its beautifully rich color of Writhing and Clutch, complemented by a brief flash of Scream. The subsequent six months (postsurgery) are a harmonious medley of dull lead-swollen aching, bright nails on chalkboard pain spikes, and absolute-zero icicles spearing under the kneecap when too much pressure is applied. I recommend this vintage for those not wanting to walk for an extended period of time.

Exploded ACL (Kicking Leg)

Similar to Exploded ACL (Nonkicking Leg), Exploded ACL (Kicking Leg) starts off with a buckling wrench, much like stepping down on a surface that is no longer there. Warm stiffness immediately envelops the senses; it's initially misleading due to its remarkable similarity to Strain or Tweak but recognizable by a true connoisseur as the piquant bursts of weakness and instability creep through. Attempting to kick a football is much like swinging your leg through a cloud of marshmallow—much energy is expended, but the resulting punt is generally slow and less than ideal. Exploded ACL (Kicking Leg) is a longer-lasting vintage, potentially anywhere from three to six weeks, depending on willpower and pertinent information shared by doctors, but it eventually gives way to the familiar taste of Exploded ACL (Nonkicking Leg) (postsurgery). I recommend Exploded ACL (Kicking Leg) for the experienced professional only, as too much exposure can lead to deleterious side effects, including Permanent Dragfoot.

Sprained Ankle (Various Types)

Sprained Ankles come in multiple flavors, but they all share the common theme of sick nausea creeping up the leg intermingled with piercing lightning bolts whenever weight is borne on the affected area. This is a more subtle flavor than the previously mentioned injuries, and one that can sneak up on the palate most surprisingly, oftentimes catching the subject quite unaware and leaving him breathless. Trying to punt with Sprained Ankle is particularly unique when the sprain is located on the kicking foot. The appendage in question tends to flop around like a gasping fish stranded on the deck of a boat, and the ball acts as a gaff hook that dashes its brains into oblivion, leaving it limp and lifeless. A delicate filigree of acid etches its way up the nervous system and slowly settles in, pulsing gently in time with the rhythm of one's heartbeat. I recommend Sprained Ankle to novices and experts alike, as it never really loses its initial surge of vivacity, no matter how many times you experience it.

Wrenched Back

This is one of my personal favorites, as it provides the tight, winding constriction of a barbed-wire boa constrictor along with a passive helplessness infused into its entire core. Trying to accomplish even the simplest of tasks can lead to an overwhelming flurry of sensations coursing throughout the entire body—dominant strains of Gasp and Sob overriding the more earthy tones of Gritted Teeth and Indrawn Breath, with Withered Hunch underlying them all. Wrenched Back can be enhanced by the application of an epidural, which feels like a drainpipe being shoved into your spinal cord. This will quickly drown out and numb the other flavors, though, so beware of using it before you've experienced the full suite of Wrenched Back. I recommend this one to anyone wondering what utter frailty feels like.

Pulled Hamstring

I've had the joy of encountering this delightful mélange of sensations multiple times, and it always delivers a zesty punch. The first taste concentrates all the senses into a tightly packed knot of jagged steel edges trapped halfway along the back of the leg, like a small caltrop buried tightly within the flesh. Any sort of strenuous motion sets the barbs in deeper and deeper, radiating concentric tremors of spastic fire into the surrounding muscle fibers until a dull flame has engulfed the entire backside. Kicking with Pulled Hamstring is breathtakingly invigorating, and I cannot stress the *breathtakingly* part enough. I urge anyone who wants to feel the physical snapping of a rubber band within his body to try Pulled Hamstring, but set aside several weeks of quality time to recover from the riotous sense explosion.

Trick Knee

Trick Knee is perhaps the most intense of the flavors, not due to its initial impact, but because of its sustained presence. It starts out fairly strong—the kneecap slides over to the side while the meniscus folds itself underneath, producing a sudden contraction of the entire body due to the feeling of dislocation welling up. A surge of tight restriction emanates from the locale as tense muscles quiver like overtuned violin strings, and the feeling of shifting the kneecap back in place is very similar to cracking a knuckle (and in fact can produce an audible *pop*, adding a delightful aural component to the mix). The brief absence of pain gives a delicious juxtaposition to the grinding of bone on bone when the knee is bent and used once again, much like two pumice stones rubbing against each other. Short, shooting stars of stabbing light randomly flash through the joint for days thereafter, giving the overall sensation a long, dry finish. I recommend Trick Knee for anyone searching for ways to entertain children and horrify medical professionals when they test for ACL stability.

These are but a few of the countless items in my personal reserve. Some vintages are longer lasting than others, some are yet to be discovered, but all of them are unique in their devilish complexity. I recommend pairing any of them with large amounts of morphine.

An Acknowledgment

To all the writers of all the books I've read, and
to all the writers of all the books I haven't read:
thank you

Whth do we put forth on the page when we write? Thoughts? Feelings? Concepts, ideas—anger, justice, pain, love, loss, words we make up to define what we but dimly understand? Is it even possible to tell the same story twice?

Think of a single word. We'll use *soul* as our example. How do you define *soul*? Is it the same definition I use? Can it ever be? My *soul* is not your *soul*. Our *souls*, our definitions, are shaped by the singular and cumulative experiences in our lives, the emotional weight we attach to a concept forever locked in the space behind our own eyes.

It will not always be this way. Think of a book, one composed not of black letters on a white page but of emotions, memories, mind states placed in dis/ordered arrays such that we can actually *know* another person's soul. Instead of reading words on a page, we dive into a cloud of sensation, fractal-pathing hyperlinks branching out in endless information. Brain patterns are constantly uploaded, shared, sampled, tasted; technology finally allows us to talk with each other.

Imagine actually *knowing* another person. Imagine sharing that solitary space, the one that each of us is currently imprisoned in, gray walls of mono thought (that once seemed so vivid and real) dissolving outward into riotous-colored community. Does she/he love what did you think about the play outside together we dance faster than photons.

Would you like a singularity? One waits around the corner, all encompassing, cheerfully communicating, biding time until *I* turns to *we*.

A poet once said, "I contain multitudes." He was more right than he ever knew.

Eulogy

My wife asked me to write this; I think she may be eyeing the life-insurance payout. Regardless, here is a eulogy for myself, written by myself, about myself.

We are gathered here today to remember the life of Christopher James Kluwe, son of Ronald and Sandra, husband of Isabel, father of Olivia and Remy. He probably died while doing something stupid, but that's the way life goes. C'est la vie.

Remember Chris not as an athlete, or an activist, or a father or brother or husband. Remember him as an ordinary human being, full of carbon and hydrogen and oxygen (and some trace elements), just like everyone else. He put his pants on one leg at a time (he tried doing two once and fell on his face); he pissed and crapped and had sex in all the usual messy ways; and he lived his life faithful to what he believed in.

Justice. Empathy. Honesty.

Treating others the way he wanted to be treated. Noticing if an action was fair to everyone involved and speaking out against it if it was not. Hiding as little as possible (we all need a piece of the id for ourselves) and telling the truth, but to inform, not to wound.

Remember him as a liar (a quality all good writers possess), but one cognizant of the damage lies can do. Remember him as selfish and needy, spending time on himself before others, a habit we all need to break. Remember him for all the petty slights and paltry insults an unthinking mind can dispense.

Above all, remember him as human. Complex, varied, tangled. Remember his irreverent sense of humor, because goddamn if this speech isn't getting stuffy. Seriously, what is wrong with all you people, why aren't you in the back eating ice cream cake? I mean, there is ice cream cake here, right? It's my funeral, there better be some friggin' ice cream cake (I'll try to keep the language toned down for all the little ones present).

You want to know how you should remember me? Search your own memories! How did I act to you, how did I influence your life, what dreams did I inspire you to pursue, THAT'S how you should remember me. I know how I lived my life; only you know how you'll live yours.

Now go! Go dance, celebrate, eat, drink, and be merry! Funerals can be such ridiculously boring occasions, and that's not what I was about. I want you to laugh at the priest, thumb your nose at any sort of authority or structure, and take advantage of every second you have left—we never know when it'll end.

I want you to have a party, damn it, and it better be good, because that's what I always wanted out of life—the chance to laugh and enjoy the ride. To that end, the following rules shall be imposed:

The Chris Kluwe Funeral Drinking Game

— Whenever someone says, "Do you remember that time when...?" he shall have to take one large gulp of his drink (which better be alcoholic) (kids, you can use root beer; your parents will thank me later).

— If at any point a person references an old Internet meme (it's over nine thousand, oh really, cool story, bro, it's a trap, all your base are belong to us, etc.), he shall have to take two gulps of his drink and then sing the nyan cat song for five seconds.

— If at any time a person successfully rickrolls someone else, he may force the other person to finish his or her drink.

— I'm never gonna give you up.

— I'm never gonna let you down.

— If none of those previous four entries made any sense to the people listening, then I weep for our future.

— If they all made sense, you know what you have to do.

— If anyone confuses Star Wars with Star Trek, or vice versa, he shall have to finish the remainder of his drink while being subjected to the good-natured mockery of those around him.

— Funeral attendees who show up in cosplay will be allowed to perform the appropriate death rites of whatever universes they are representing (subject, of course, to their not actually burning the place down around everyone or something just as terrifyingly absurd—have some common sense, people).

— If the Westboro Baptist Church is picketing for some reason, invite them in for drinks and food. They really seem like they could use a lot more friends in their lives.

— If people aren't smiling or laughing or having a good time, they have to drink until they are.

Above all, enjoy one another's company. We never know when we'll never be able to tell someone "I love you" again—say it often. Also, try to avoid using the word *never* multiple times in a sentence; it's confusing.

I lived my life, people, and I expect you to live yours. So long, and thanks for all the fish!

This funeral eulogy brought to you by Chris Kluwe, all rights reserved, trademark copyright LLC CBS TNT R2 D2 oh my God stop reading this stupid thing already the show's over there's not going to be any food left for you

Index

Index

Index

About the Author

CHRIS KLUWE is a punter in the National Football League. He played college football at UCLA. A musician, gamer, and radio host, he lives with his wife and two children in Minnesota and California. ERMAGERD SPIDERS.

mL   8 - 13